Appetizer Appeal

Member Recipes

Cooking Club of America

Minnetonka · Minnesota

Appetizer Appeal
Member Recipes

Printed in 2011.

Tom Carpenter
Creative Director

Jen Weaverling
Managing Editor

Wendy Holdman
Cover Design

Susan Telleen
Recipe Editor and Food Stylist Assistant

Zachary Marell
Book Design and Production

Phil Aarrestad
Commissioned Photography

Robin Krause
Abby Wykcoff
Food Stylists

Susan Hammes
Prop Stylist

John Keenan
Photo Assistant

On Cover: *Tandoori Chicken Tidbits, page 22.*
On Back Cover: *Spinach Quichelets, page 70.*
Pesto Eggs with Shrimp, page 113.
Crab Dip, page 56.

3 4 5 6 / 15 14 13 12 11
© 2010 Cooking Club of America
ISBN 13: 978-1-58159-479-9

Special thanks to: Elizabeth Pomroy and Ruth Petran.

Cooking Club of America
12301 Whitewater Drive
Minnetonka, MN 55343
www.cookingclub.com

Contents

Give all your events some *Appetizer Appeal!*

Gatherings, get-togethers, open-houses, holidays, special dinners, parties ... events of all kinds call for appetizers. Of course, appetizers themselves go by a variety of names too: *hors d'oeuvres,* snacks, finger food, munchies, bites, warm-ups and more. And once you've decided what to call them, the variety of appetizers you can create is almost endless: dips, salsas, canapés, pizzas, breads, spreads, sandwiches, crostini, wraps, roll-ups, folds and so many others. Here's an opportunity to expand your recipe repertoire when it comes to foods like these — tasteful delights that are leading the way toward dinner or occupying family and friends' hands (and tastebuds) at any gathering. We went to one of the best sources we know — Cooking Club of America members — to gather these appetizing delights. So whether you and your guests are browsing, grazing, noshing, snacking or just warming up, consider this your official guidebook to *Appetizer Appeal!*

Chicken, Seafood & Meat Bites

CHESAPEAKE BAY CRAB CAKES WITH JALAPENO TARTAR SAUCE

DAVID HEPPNER
BRANDON, FLORIDA

CAKES

1 large egg, lightly beaten

2 tablespoons reduced-fat mayonnaise

2 tablespoons finely chopped green bell pepper

1 (2-oz.) jar diced pimientos, drained

1½ tablespoons finely chopped red onion

1½ teaspoons fresh lemon juice

1 teaspoon Dijon mustard

½ teaspoon seafood seasoning

½ cup fresh whole-grain bread crumbs

1 lb. canned lump crabmeat, drained, flaked

SAUCE

½ cup reduced-fat mayonnaise

1 small jalapeño chile, seeded, finely chopped

3 tablespoons finely chopped unpeeled English cucumber

2 tablespoons finely chopped red onion

1 tablespoon fresh lemon juice

¼ teaspoon Worcestershire sauce

❶ In large bowl, combine egg, 2 tablespoons mayonnaise, bell pepper, pimientos, 1½ tablespoons onion, 1½ teaspoons lemon juice, mustard and seafood seasoning; mix well. Fold in bread crumbs and crabmeat. Divide crabmeat mixture into 12 portions; shape each portion into 1-inch-thick patty.

❷ Spray large skillet with nonstick cooking spray. Heat skillet over medium-high heat until hot. Add crab cakes; cook 3 to 4 minutes, turning once, until golden brown and thoroughly cooked.

❸ In another large bowl, combine ½ cup mayonnaise, chile, cucumber, 2 tablespoons onion, 1 tablespoon lemon juice and Worcestershire sauce; mix well. Refrigerate, covered, 1 hour or until chilled. Serve crab cakes with sauce.

4 servings.

SHRIMP PUFFS WITH MUSTARD SAUCE

ANN NACE
PERKASIE, PENNSYLVANIA

PUFFS

1 lb. shelled, deveined uncooked small shrimp, finely chopped

10 water chestnuts, finely chopped

1 tablespoon cornstarch

1 teaspoon sweet white wine

½ teaspoon salt

1 egg, beaten

¼ cup canola oil

MUSTARD SAUCE

½ cup dry mustard

½ cup water

2½ tablespoons sugar

❶ In large bowl, combine shrimp, water chestnuts, cornstarch, wine, salt and egg; mix well. Form mixture into 1½-inch balls.

❷ In large skillet, heat oil over medium-high heat until hot. Add shrimp balls; fry until golden brown outside and shrimp turns pink. Drain on paper towels.

❸ In small bowl, combine mustard, water and sugar; blend until smooth. Serve with shrimp balls.

8 servings.

TANGY LIME WINGS

CAROLE RESNICK
CLEVELAND, OHIO

3 lb. chicken wings, separated at joints, tips discarded

1 cup fresh orange juice

3/4 cup chopped fresh cilantro

1 cup lime marmalade

1/2 cup olive oil

1/2 cup fresh lime juice

2 tablespoons freshly ground pepper

3 garlic cloves, minced

2 tablespoons steak sauce

1 tablespoon Worcestershire sauce

2 teaspoons salt

2 teaspoons grated lime peel

2 limes, cut into wedges

Fresh cilantro sprigs

❶ Place chicken wings in 3-quart glass casserole.

❷ In medium bowl, combine orange juice, cilantro, 1/2 cup marmalade, oil, 1/4 cup lime juice, pepper, garlic, steak sauce, Worcestershire sauce, salt and 1 teaspoon of the lime peel; mix well. Pour half of the marinade over the wings; cover and reserve remaining marinade in refrigerator. Refrigerate wings, covered, 1 hour, turning once.

❸ Heat oven to 350°F.

❹ Remove reserved marinade from refrigerator. Strain into medium saucepan. Boil 5 minutes over medium-high heat or until reduced by half, stirring occasionally. Add remaining 1/2 cup marmalade, 1/4 cup lime juice and 1 teaspoon lime peel; boil an additional 1 minute.

❺ Remove chicken from refrigerator. Drain and discard marinade. Place wings in clean 3-quart casserole. Pour half of the boiled marinade over wings. Bake 30 minutes, turning and basting frequently with marinade.

❻ Heat broiler. Broil wings 6 inches from heat about 1 minute, turning once, until crisp, golden and juices run clear. Transfer wings to serving platter. Garnish with lime wedges and cilantro sprigs.

10 servings.

CALICO SCALLOPS

JENNIFER RUBINO
HICKORY, NORTH CAROLINA

1 lb. calico or bay scallops

3 tablespoons melted butter

3 tablespoons freshly grated Parmesan cheese

2 green onions, thinly sliced

Seafood seasoning

❶ Heat broiler. Rinse and drain scallops. Arrange scallops on broiler pan; brush with melted butter. Sprinkle cheese and onions over scallops. Lightly dust with seafood seasoning. Broil 8 inches from heat 4 to 5 minutes or until scallops are opaque. Serve hot.

5 servings.

ZESTY SAUSAGE APPETIZERS

ALBERTA DEVRIES
PELLA, IOWA

3/4 cup packed brown sugar

3 tablespoons cornstarch

1/4 cup fresh lemon juice

Juice from 1 (10-oz.) jar maraschino cherries

Juice from 1 (13-oz.) can pineapple chunks

2 lb. small sausage links

1 green bell pepper, diced

1/4 teaspoon salt

❶ In large saucepan, combine brown sugar, cornstarch, lemon juice, cherry juice and pineapple juice; mix well. Cook over medium heat until mixture thickens. Add sausage, bell pepper and salt; heat through. Serve in slow cooker.

24 servings.

HONEY-MUSTARD TURKEY MEATBALLS

PEGGY YAMAGUCHI-LAZAR
EUGENE, OREGON

1 lb. ground turkey breast

1 large egg, lightly beaten

3/4 cup crushed reduced-fat butter-flavored crackers

1/2 cup shredded part-skim mozzarella cheese

1/4 cup chopped onions

1/2 teaspoon ground ginger

1 tablespoon dried parsley

1/2 teaspoon freshly ground pepper

6 tablespoons Dijon mustard

1 1/4 cups orange juice or unsweetened pineapple juice

1/4 cup chopped green bell peppers

2 tablespoons honey

1 tablespoon cornstarch

1/4 teaspoon onion powder or garlic powder

❶ Heat oven to 350°F. Spray 13x9-inch pan with nonstick cooking spray.

❷ In large bowl, combine turkey, egg, cracker crumbs, cheese, onions, ginger, parsley, pepper and 3 tablespoons of the mustard; mix well. Shape mixture into 30 (1-inch) meatballs. Arrange meatballs 1 inch apart on pan. Bake 20 to 25 minutes or until juices run clear. Set aside and keep warm.

❸ In large saucepan, bring orange juice, bell peppers, honey, cornstarch and onion powder to a boil over medium heat, stirring constantly. Reduce heat; stir in remaining 3 tablespoons mustard until smooth. Brush meatballs with about 1/4 cup sauce. Bake an additional 10 minutes. Serve remaining dipping sauce with meatballs.

10 servings.

SOMALIAN MOUSHKAKI WITH TOMATO RELISH

ROSEMARY JOHNSON
IRONDALE, ALABAMA

MOUSHKAKI

1 1/2 lb. beef round steak or London broil, cut into 1-inch cubes

2 onions, cut into 1-inch squares

1 teaspoon cayenne pepper

1 teaspoon garlic salt

3 garlic cloves, minced

1 tablespoon minced fresh ginger

1 teaspoon minced tarragon

3 tablespoons fresh lime juice

3 tablespoons olive oil

TOMATO RELISH

1 onion, chopped

1 small green bell pepper, chopped

6 plum tomatoes, chopped

1/4 cup sugar

1/2 cup raspberry vinegar

1 teaspoon kosher (coarse) salt

1 teaspoon fennel seed, crushed

1/2 teaspoon ground allspice

1/2 teaspoon cinnamon

1/4 teaspoon whole cloves

❶ Place steak and onions in 3-quart casserole.

❷ In small bowl, combine cayenne, garlic salt, garlic, ginger, tarragon, lime juice and oil; mix well. Pour mixture over steak and onions. Refrigerate, covered, at least 6 hours or overnight.

❸ Heat grill. Soak 12 (6-inch) bamboo skewers in water 30 minutes; drain skewers. Alternately thread meat cubes and onion chunks onto skewers. Place skewers on gas grill over high heat or on charcoal grill 4 to 6 inches from hot coals. Cook 3 to 5 minutes per side or until browned and of desired doneness.

❹ In large saucepan, heat onion, bell pepper, tomatoes and sugar over medium heat. Cook 10 to 15 minutes or until mixture thickens. Stir in vinegar, salt, fennel seed, allspice, cinnamon and cloves; cook an additional 10 minutes. Remove from heat; cool. Serve hot with relish.

6 servings.

SOMALIAN MOUSHKAKI WITH TOMATO RELISH

SNACK-SIZE BARBECUED RIBS

ANNIE KIRKENDALL
KANSAS CITY, KANSAS

2 lb. pork ribs

2 tablespoons butter

4 green onions, chopped

1 tablespoon all-purpose flour

1 tablespoon Dijon mustard

1 cup canned reduced-sodium beef broth

2 tablespoons fresh lemon juice

3 tablespoons chili sauce

❶ Heat oven to 450°F. Cut ribs into 2- or 3-rib portions. Arrange in single layer in 3-quart casserole. Bake 20 minutes; drain.

❷ Meanwhile, melt butter in medium skillet over medium-high heat. Add green onions; sauté 3 minutes. Stir in flour and mustard. Cook, stirring frequently, 2 minutes.

❸ Gradually stir in broth, lemon juice and chili sauce. Cook 5 minutes, stirring constantly.

❹ Brush sauce over ribs. Bake an additional 25 minutes or until ribs are tender, turning and basting occasionally with sauce.

8 servings.

PARTY WINGS

GEORGIA NUA
PALM SPRINGS, CALIFORNIA

3 tablespoons cider vinegar

2 tablespoons low-sodium soy sauce

1/3 cup pineapple juice

2 tablespoons vegetable oil

2 teaspoons prepared horseradish

1 large garlic clove, minced

3 lb. chicken wings, separated at joints, tips discarded

❶ In large bowl, combine vinegar, soy sauce, pineapple juice, oil, horseradish and garlic; mix well. Reserve 1/4 of the marinade; cover and refrigerate. Add chicken wings to remaining marinade. Refrigerate, covered, at least 1 hour or overnight.

❷ Heat oven to 425°F. Remove chicken from marinade; discard marinade. Place chicken in 13x9-inch pan; pour reserved marinade over the chicken. Bake 50 to 60 minutes, turning occasionally, or until chicken is no longer pink in center and juices run clear.

10 servings.

SHRIMP SALAD

CAROL CROSTON
HEMPSTEAD, NEW YORK

1 (12-oz.) bag shelled, deveined cooked small shrimp, cut into bite-size pieces

1 (6-oz.) pkg. cooked crabmeat, cut into bite-size pieces

1 rib celery, diced

1/8 cup coarsely chopped onions

1 small cabbage, diced

1 medium carrot, diced

1/8 teaspoon seasoned salt

1/8 teaspoon freshly ground pepper

1/4 cup Italian dressing

1/2 cup mayonnaise

❶ In large bowl, combine shrimp, crab, celery, onions, cabbage, carrot, seasoned salt, pepper, dressing and mayonnaise; mix well. Refrigerate, covered, 2 hours or until chilled before serving.

12 servings.

CHICKEN SALAD

BERNICE SCHUMANN
NEW BRAUNFELS, TEXAS

1 cup mayonnaise

1 tablespoon Dijon mustard

1 tablespoon packed brown sugar

5 cups diced cooked chicken

2 large apples, cored, diced

1 cup thinly sliced celery

½ to 1 cup chopped walnuts

Lettuce leaves or cream puff shells

❶ In medium bowl, combine mayonnaise, mustard and brown sugar; mix well. Stir in chicken, apples, celery and walnuts. Refrigerate, covered, at least 2 hours. Serve on lettuce leaves or in cream puff shells.

16 servings.

JUMBO SHRIMP AND MARINADE

JULIE MARTINEZ
CARMICHAEL, CALIFORNIA

12 shelled, deveined uncooked jumbo shrimp

1 garlic clove, minced

2 oranges, halved

¼ cup olive oil

❶ In medium bowl, combine shrimp and garlic. Squeeze oranges over shrimp, making sure shrimp are submerged in juice. Refrigerate, covered, 4 hours.

❷ In large skillet, heat oil over medium-high heat until hot. Remove shrimp from marinade; discard marinade. Cook shrimp 4 to 6 minutes, turning occasionally, until shrimp turn pink.

6 servings.

MINI CRAB COCKTAIL CAKES

BARBARA BRANDEL
LAKELAND, FLORIDA

CRAB CAKES

1 lb. canned lump crabmeat, drained, flaked

2 egg whites, lightly beaten

¼ cup sour cream

½ cup chopped green onions

1 tablespoon fresh lemon juice

1 cup fresh whole-grain bread crumbs

2 teaspoons fresh dill or 1 teaspoon dried

SAUCE

1 cup sour cream

½ cup chopped green onions

❶ Heat oven to 375°F.

❷ In large bowl, combine crabmeat, egg whites, ¼ cup sour cream, ½ cup green onions and lemon juice; mix well. Form mixture into 1-inch-thick patties.

❸ In medium bowl, combine bread crumbs and dill. Roll crab cakes in crumb mixture. Arrange cakes on 13x9-inch pan. Bake 10 to 15 minutes or until golden brown.

❹ In small bowl, combine 1 cup sour cream and ½ cup green onions; mix well. Serve with hot crab cakes.

12 servings.

COCONUT SHRIMP WITH PINEAPPLE DIPPING SAUCE

COCONUT SHRIMP WITH PINEAPPLE DIPPING SAUCE

ANITA COYNE
BONITA SPRINGS, FLORIDA

SHRIMP
½ cup all-purpose flour
1 teaspoon dry mustard
1 teaspoon salt
1 egg, beaten
½ cup coconut cream
1 cup flaked coconut
⅔ cup dry bread crumbs
1 lb. shelled, deveined uncooked large shrimp, tails on

SAUCE
⅔ cup pineapple preserves
¼ cup prepared horseradish
1 tablespoon fresh lemon juice
¼ teaspoon freshly ground pepper

❶ In small bowl, combine flour, mustard and salt; set aside.

❷ In medium bowl, combine egg and coconut cream; mix until well blended.

❸ In another medium bowl, combine coconut with bread crumbs. Dredge shrimp in flour mixture, then cream mixture and coconut mixture. Refrigerate, covered, until well chilled.

❹ Heat broiler. Broil shrimp 3 to 5 minutes per side, turning once, until shrimp turn pink. Drain on paper towels.

❺ In medium bowl, combine preserves, horseradish, lemon juice and pepper; mix well. Refrigerate, covered, until chilled. Serve dipping sauce with shrimp.

12 servings.

PROSCIUTTO-WRAPPED SCAMPI

SAGE BERTON
FAIRFAX, CALIFORNIA

12 shelled, deveined uncooked jumbo shrimp
½ cup dry white wine
½ cup olive oil
2 garlic cloves, minced
¼ teaspoon crushed red pepper
3 thin prosciutto slices, halved lengthwise, halved crosswise
2 tablespoons minced fresh Italian parsley
Lemon wedges

❶ In large bowl, combine wine, oil, garlic and red pepper; mix well. Reserve ¼ of the marinade; refrigerate. Add shrimp to remaining marinade; toss to coat. Refrigerate, covered, 1 hour.

❷ Heat broiler. Remove shrimp from marinade; discard marinade. Wrap 1 slice prosciutto around each shrimp. Arrange 3 shrimp in each of 4 shallow broiler-proof dishes, tucking ends of prosciutto strips under shrimp. Drizzle 1 tablespoon of the reserved marinade over shrimp in each dish.

❸ Broil shrimp 6 inches from heat 4 to 6 minutes, turning once, until prosciutto begins to crisp and shrimp turn pink. Sprinkle with parsley. Serve with lemon wedges.

4 servings.

SWEET 'N SPICY SMOKIES

CAROL HAWLEY
FREDERICK, MARYLAND

1 cup ketchup
½ cup grape jelly
1 to 2 tablespoons diced jalapeño chiles
1 (1-lb.) pkg. cocktail smoked sausages
1 (8-oz.) can crushed pineapple in juice, undrained

❶ In medium saucepan, combine ketchup, jelly and chiles. Cook and stir over medium heat until well blended. Add sausages and pineapple; cook until hot. Serve in chafing dish or keep warm in slow cooker.

4 servings.

CHICKEN SALAD BALLS

PATRICIA ANNE SMITH
NEBO, NORTH CAROLINA

1 cup cooked finely shredded chicken
1 tablespoon finely chopped onion
Dash of hot pepper sauce
½ cup salad dressing or mayonnaise
1 tablespoon Dijon mustard
2 cups ground pecans
2 tablespoons pickle relish, well drained
2 tablespoons chopped pimientos, well drained
2 tablespoons chopped ripe olives

❶ In large bowl, combine chicken, onion, hot pepper sauce, salad dressing, mustard, 1 cup of the pecans, pickle relish, pimiento and olives; mix well. Refrigerate, covered, at least 2 hours.

❷ Shape mixture into 1-inch balls, then roll in remaining 1 cup ground pecans.

10 servings.

PANCETTA-WRAPPED SCALLOPS WITH LEMON

PEGGY WINKWORTH
DURANGO, COLORADO

12 large sea scallops, membrane removed, halved
3 tablespoons extra-virgin olive oil
Peel of 1 lemon, plus 1 teaspoon finely grated peel
2 fresh rosemary sprigs
⅛ teaspoon freshly ground pepper
12 thin slices pancetta, halved
1 teaspoon finely chopped rosemary

❶ In medium bowl, toss scallops with oil, lemon strips, rosemary sprigs and pepper. Refrigerate, covered, 2 hours.

❷ Heat broiler. Remove scallops from marinade; discard marinade. Lightly pat scallops dry.

❸ Wrap each scallop piece in slice of pancetta; secure with toothpick. Place on broiler pan. Broil 4 to 6 inches from heat about 1 to 2 minutes per side, turning once, until pancetta sizzles and scallops are firm and opaque but not rubbery.

❹ In small bowl, combine grated lemon peel and chopped rosemary. Dip each wrapped scallop in lemon-herb mixture before serving.

8 servings.

PANCETTA-WRAPPED SCALLOPS WITH LEMON

BUFFALO SHRIMP

DEBBIE BYRNE
CLINTON, CONNECTICUT

1 large egg, beaten

½ cup milk

1 cup all-purpose flour

1 lb. shelled, deveined uncooked large shrimp, butterflied

¼ cup vegetable oil

¼ cup butter

¼ cup hot pepper sauce

Dash of freshly ground pepper

Dash of garlic powder

⅛ teaspoon paprika

½ cup blue cheese salad dressing

❶ In small bowl, combine egg and milk. Place flour in another small bowl.

❷ Dip each shrimp in egg mixture, then dredge in flour, making sure to coat evenly. Refrigerate 10 minutes before frying.

❸ In large skillet, heat oil over medium-high heat until hot. Add shrimp; cook 4 to 6 minutes or until shrimp turn pink. Drain on paper towels.

❹ In small saucepan, combine butter, hot pepper sauce, black pepper, garlic powder and paprika. Cook, stirring occasionally, over low heat until butter is melted and ingredients are well blended.

❺ Combine fried shrimp and hot sauce mixture until coated. Serve immediately with blue cheese dressing.

4 servings.

ZESTY CHICKEN WINGS

CHRIS McBEE
XENIA, OHIO

½ cup corn syrup

½ cup ketchup

¼ cup cider vinegar

¼ cup Worcestershire sauce

¼ cup Dijon mustard

1 small onion, chopped

3 garlic cloves, minced

1 tablespoon chili powder

16 whole chicken wings (about 3 lb.), separated at joints, tips discarded

❶ In large saucepan, combine corn syrup, ketchup, vinegar, Worcestershire sauce, mustard, onion, garlic and chili powder. Bring to a boil over medium-high heat. Reduce heat to medium; simmer, uncovered, 15 to 20 minutes or until thickened. Toss wings with ½ of the sauce. Reserve remaining sauce for dipping.

❷ Heat oven to 375°F.

❸ Spray 15x10x1-inch baking pan with nonstick cooking spray. Arrange wings in pan. Bake 20 to 25 minutes or until juices run clear, turning once. Serve with reserved sauce.

10 servings.

DEVILED HAM BITES

CHARLOTTE WARD
HILTON HEAD ISLAND, SOUTH CAROLINA

1 (3-oz.) pkg. cream cheese, softened

½ cup (2 oz.) blue cheese, crumbled

1 (2 ⅓-oz.) can deviled ham

¼ cup chopped pecans

¼ teaspoon onion juice

½ cup minced fresh parsley

24 thin pretzel sticks

❶ In medium bowl, combine cream cheese, blue cheese, ham, pecans and onion juice; mix well. Refrigerate, covered, until firm. Shape mixture into 1-inch balls, then roll in parlsey. Refrigerate, covered, again until firm.

❷ Insert 1 pretzel stick into each ball before serving.

12 servings.

SUCCULENT CRAB CAKES

VICKI WILLIAMSON
BELLINGHAM, WASHINGTON

1 egg, beaten
1 lb. canned lump crabmeat, drained, flaked
1 cup mayonnaise
½ teaspoon dry mustard
¼ cup chopped green bell peppers
2 green onions, chopped
¼ cup (1 oz.) finely shredded Swiss cheese
1 cup unsalted cracker crumbs
¼ cup canola oil

❶ In large bowl, combine egg, crabmeat, mayonnaise, mustard, bell peppers and green onions; mix well. Stir in cheese. Shape mixture into small balls, then roll in cracker crumbs.

❷ In large skillet, heat oil over medium-high heat until hot. Add crab cakes; fry 4 to 6 minutes or until golden brown.

20 servings.

GOLDEN CHICKEN NUGGETS

GLENDA CAVANAH
RUSSELLVILLE, KENTUCKY

½ cup fine dry bread crumbs
¼ cup (1 oz.) freshly grated Parmesan cheese
2 teaspoons seasoned salt
1 teaspoon salt
1 teaspoon dried thyme
1 teaspoon dried basil
¼ teaspoon chopped fresh parsley
4 boneless skinless chicken breasts, cut into 1-inch pieces
½ cup melted butter

❶ Heat oven to 400°F. Line baking sheet with aluminum foil.

❷ In large bowl, combine bread crumbs, cheese, seasoned salt, salt, thyme, basil and parsley; mix well. Dip chicken into butter, then roll in crumb mixture.

❸ Place chicken on baking sheet. Bake 10 minutes or until chicken is no longer pink in center.

30 servings.

COCKTAIL MEATBALLS

DAWN NEUSIUS
FERNDALE, MICHIGAN

MEATBALLS
1 lb. ground beef
1 lb. ground pork
1½ cups fine dry bread crumbs or crushed saltines
4 large eggs
¼ cup diced green and red bell peppers
2 tablespoons hot pepper sauce
½ teaspoon garlic salt
¼ teaspoon salt

SAUCE
1½ cups ketchup
1 cup water
½ cup vinegar
⅔ cup packed brown sugar
2 teaspoons mustard
1 tablespoon salt
2 tablespoons Worcestershire sauce
1 tablespoon hot pepper sauce

❶ Heat oven to 325°F.

❷ In large bowl, combine beef, pork, bread crumbs, eggs, bell peppers, 2 tablespoons hot pepper sauce, garlic salt and ¼ teaspoon salt; mix well. With hands, shape mixture into 1-inch meatballs. Arrange meatballs 1 inch apart on baking sheet. Bake 30 minutes or until no longer pink in center.

❸ In medium bowl, combine ketchup, water, vinegar, brown sugar, mustard, 1 tablespoon salt, Worcestershire sauce and 1 tablespoon hot pepper sauce; mix well.

❹ Remove meatballs from oven; transfer to 3-quart casserole. Pour ketchup mixture over meatballs. Bake an additional 1 hour.

22 servings.

SMOKED SALMON STACKS

SMOKED SALMON STACKS

BARBARA ASCHENBRENNER
LOS ALTOS, CALIFORNIA

1 tablespoon butter

2 leeks (white and pale green parts only), coarsely chopped

½ (8-oz.) pkg. cream cheese, softened

1 to 2 teaspoons prepared horseradish

2 tablespoons whipping cream

6 oz. thinly sliced smoked salmon (1x6-inch pieces)

Lettuce leaves

❶ In small skillet, melt butter over medium-high heat. Add leeks; sauté 5 minutes or until tender.

❷ In medium bowl, combine cream cheese, leeks, horseradish and cream; mix to spreading consistency.

❸ Place salmon strip on work surface. Spread 2 teaspoons cream cheese mixture over salmon; top with another salmon strip, cream cheese and third salmon strip. Repeat with remaining salmon and cream cheese mixture. Wrap stacks in plastic wrap; refrigerate until chilled.

❹ Remove salmon stacks from plastic wrap; cut each stack into 6 (1-inch) squares. Arrange squares over lettuce leaves on serving platter.

6 servings.

TERIYAKI CHICKEN WINGS

ALICE BLAKE
FORT STEWART, GEORGIA

MARINADE

½ cup low-sodium soy sauce

¼ cup packed brown sugar

1 tablespoon finely chopped garlic

½ teaspoon cayenne pepper

¼ cup water

1 tablespoon sesame oil

CHICKEN

20 chicken wings, tips discarded

2 tablespoons sesame seeds

❶ In small saucepan, combine soy sauce, brown sugar, garlic, cayenne and water. Bring to a boil over medium-high heat, stirring to dissolve sugar. Remove from heat; cool to room temperature. Gradually stir in oil.

❷ Place wings in large resealable plastic bag; add half of the marinade. Refrigerate remaining marinade. Seal bag; turn to evenly coat wings. Refrigerate at least 1 hour or up to 4 hours, turning bag occasionally.

❸ Heat grill. Remove wings from marinade; discard marinade. Sprinkle wings with sesame seeds. Place wings on gas grill over medium heat or on charcoal grill 4 to 6 inches from medium coals. Cook, 14 to 15 minutes, basting occasionally with reserved marinade until chicken is no longer pink in center and juices run clear.

10 servings.

CRAB POLENTA WITH HORSERADISH CREAM

CONSTANCE ZECCHIN
TUCSON, ARIZONA

POLENTA

2 cups canned reduced-sodium chicken broth

2 cups whipping cream

1 cup polenta meal or yellow cornmeal

1/2 cup all-purpose flour

2 (6-oz.) cans lump crabmeat, drained, flaked

1 cup (4 oz.) grated Edam cheese

1/4 cup butter

HORSERADISH CREAM

1 (8-oz.) container sour cream

1 tablespoon prepared horseradish

1 tablespoon dry mustard

2 teaspoons dried dill weed

❶ In medium saucepan, bring broth and cream to a boil over medium-high heat. Gradually whisk in polenta and flour; cook mixture 10 to 12 minutes, whisking constantly, until thickened. Remove from heat. Stir in crabmeat and cheese.

❷ Pour mixture into greased 9x5-inch loaf pan. Refrigerate 8 hours. Unmold; cut into 1/2-inch slices. Cut each slice into 2x1-inch rectangles.

❸ In large skillet, melt 2 tablespoons of the butter over medium heat. Add about half of the polenta slices to skillet, being careful not to crowd. Cook 3 to 4 minutes or until lightly browned, turning once; transfer to paper towels. Add remaining butter and repeat with remaining slices.

❹ In large bowl, combine sour cream, horseradish, mustard and dill weed; mix well. Refrigerate, covered, 30 minutes. Serve with polenta slices.

24 servings.

GLAZED SAUSAGE BALLS

MICHAEL DAVIS
WHEELING, WEST VIRGINIA

SAUSAGE BALLS

5 oz. bulk sausage

12 oz. ground beef

1/2 teaspoon salt

1/2 teaspoon dry mustard

1/2 teaspoon crushed coriander

1/4 teaspoon ground allspice

1 egg, beaten

1/4 cup dry bread crumbs

1/4 cup minced onions

GLAZE

1/2 cup apple jelly

1/2 cup chutney

1 teaspoon fresh lemon juice

❶ Heat oven to 500°F. Spray 13x9-inch pan with nonstick cooking spray.

❷ In large bowl, combine sausage, beef, salt, mustard, coriander, allspice, egg, bread crumbs and onions; mix well. Shape mixture into 1-inch meatballs. Arrange meatballs 1 inch apart on pan. Bake 8 to 10 minutes or until browned and no longer pink inside.

❸ Meanwhile, in large saucepan, combine jelly, chutney and lemon juice; mix well. Heat jelly mixture over medium heat until jelly melts. Add cooked meatballs; toss to glaze.

20 servings.

PEANUT CHICKEN BALLS

NANCY GARCIA
NICEVILLE, FLORIDA

2½ cups ground chicken

½ cup grated carrots

½ cup chopped fresh parsley

½ cup finely chopped onions

¾ cup mayonnaise

1½ cups dry roasted nuts, ground (peanuts, almonds or pecans)

¼ cup butter, melted

❶ Heat oven to 400°F.

❷ In large bowl, combine chicken, carrots, parsley and onions; mix well. Stir in mayonnaise; mix well. Roll mixture into 1-inch balls, then roll into ground nuts. Dip one side in butter.

❸ Arrange balls, butter side up, on 13x9-inch pan. Bake 15 minutes or until chicken is no longer pink in center. Cool before serving.

20 servings.

BACON ROLL-UPS

JENNIFER LYDDANE
WILLIAMSBURG, VIRGINIA

¼ cup butter

½ cup water

1½ cups herb-seasoned stuffing

1 egg, beaten

¼ lb. hot sausage

½ lb. thick-sliced bacon, cut into thirds

❶ In small saucepan, melt butter in water over medium heat.

❷ In large bowl, stir butter mixture into stuffing. Add egg and sausage; mix thoroughly. Shape mixture into 1-inch balls; refrigerate, covered, 1 hour. Wrap 1 piece bacon around each ball; secure with toothpick.

❸ Heat oven to 375°F.

❹ Place roll-ups on 15x10x1-inch baking pan. Cook 35 minutes, turning once after 15 minutes, until bacon is crisp and sausage is no longer pink in center. Remove roll-ups from oven. Drain on paper towels.

10 servings.

CHICKEN SENSATIONS

CHARLOTTE WARD
HILTON HEAD ISLAND, SOUTH CAROLINA

1½ to 2 cups finely crushed dry stuffing mix (use blender to crush ½ cup at a time)

1 (8-oz.) container sour cream

2 teaspoons fresh lemon juice

2 teaspoons Worcestershire sauce

1 teaspoon celery salt

½ teaspoon garlic salt

Dash of freshly ground pepper

6 boneless skinless chicken breast halves, cut into 1½-inch pieces

½ cup butter, melted

½ teaspoon paprika

❶ Heat oven to 350°F. Line 13x9-inch pan with aluminum foil; spray foil with nonstick cooking spray.

❷ Place stuffing crumbs in 9-inch pie plate. In another 9-inch pie plate, combine sour cream, lemon juice, Worcestershire sauce, celery salt, garlic salt and pepper. Dip chicken pieces in sour cream mixture, then roll in stuffing mix.

❸ Arrange chicken pieces on prepared pan. Drizzle with melted butter; sprinkle with paprika.

❹ Bake 35 to 40 minutes or until chicken is no longer pink in center and juices run clear.

16 servings.

SHRIMP AND PEA PODS

KATELYNN WILCHER
MOORESVILLE, INDIANA

1 lb. shelled, deveined uncooked medium shrimp

1 teaspoon liquid shrimp and crab boil

2 tablespoons tarragon vinegar

¼ cup sesame oil

2 garlic cloves, minced

1 (2-inch) piece fresh ginger, minced

⅛ teaspoon salt

⅛ teaspoon freshly ground pepper

18 fresh pea pods

❶ In medium saucepan, boil shrimp and crab boil over medium-high heat, in enough water to cover, until shrimp turn pink. Remove shrimp from saucepan; rinse with cold water until cool.

❷ In medium bowl, whisk together vinegar, oil, garlic, ginger, salt and pepper until well blended. Pour mixture over shrimp; stir to coat evenly. Refrigerate, covered, overnight.

❸ Blanch pea pods in boiling water 30 seconds. Plunge into ice water until cooled. Split pea pods lengthwise. Wrap 1 peapod piece around each shrimp; secure with toothpick. Refrigerate until ready to serve.

6 servings.

SWEET AND SOUR KIELBASA

JEAN WETHEREL
LUDLOW, MASSACHUSETTS

2 (1 lb.) polish sausages

1 (12-oz.) bottle red Russian dressing

1 (1-oz.) pkg. dry onion soup mix

1 (6-oz.) can apricot preserves

❶ In medium saucepan, boil sausages over medium-high heat 20 minutes. Drain sausages; cut into 1½-inch pieces.

❷ In slow cooker, combine dressing, soup mix and apricot preserves. Stir in sausage; cook 2 hours on low heat, stirring occasionally.

10 servings.

TANDOORI CHICKEN TIDBITS

GWEN CAMPBELL
STERLING, VIRGINIA

CHICKEN

4 boneless skinless chicken breast halves, quartered

½ lemon

¼ teaspoon salt

MASALA

¼ teaspoon crushed garlic

¼ teaspoon grated fresh ginger

¼ teaspoon ground coriander

¼ teaspoon paprika

¼ teaspoon ground cumin

1¼ teaspoon tumeric

1 cup plain yogurt

❶ Line 13x9-inch pan with aluminum foil.

❷ Rub each chicken piece with lemon half; sprinkle with salt.

❸ In large bowl, combine garlic, ginger, coriander, paprika, cumin, tumeric and yogurt; mix well. Reserve half of the mixture; refrigerate. Add chicken to bowl. Refrigerate, covered, 30 minutes.

❹ Heat oven to 400°F. Remove chicken from marinade; discard marinade. Place chicken on pan. Bake 35 minutes or until chicken is no longer pink in center.

❺ Remove chicken to serving platter. Insert toothpick into each piece. Or, serve on skewers. Place reserved masala in bowl to accompany chicken for dipping sauce.

8 servings.

MARINATED SHRIMP

MARY JOHNSON
STONEHAM, MASSACHUSETTS

3 lb. shelled, deveined cooked large shrimp

2 lemons, thinly sliced

2 onions, thinly sliced

2 cups sliced pitted ripe olives

2 (2-oz.) jars chopped pimientos

1 1/2 to 2 cups fresh lemon juice

3/4 cup vegetable oil

1 1/2 tablespoons wine vinegar

1 1/2 teaspoons salt

1 teaspoon freshly ground pepper

1/2 teaspoon cayenne pepper

1/2 teaspoon dry mustard

2 bay leaves, crumbled

❶ In large bowl, combine shrimp, lemons, onions, olives and pimientos.

❷ In clean, medium jar, combine lemon juice, oil, vinegar, salt, pepper, cayenne, mustard and bay leaves. Cover jar; shake well to combine. Pour lemon mixture over shrimp mixture; toss. Refrigerate, covered, 24 hours. Serve cold.

4 servings.

ORIENTAL MEATBALLS

CAROLYN LYONS
BROCKTON, MASSACHUSETTS

1/2 lb. shelled, deveined uncooked jumbo shrimp, chopped

1/2 lb. uncooked lean pork, chopped

1/2 cup chopped celery, leaves on

1/4 cup chopped green onions

1 (8-oz.) can water chestnuts, drained

2 eggs, lightly beaten

1 1/2 tablespoons low-sodium soy sauce

1/2 cup fresh bread crumbs

1/2 teaspoon salt

1/2 teaspoon freshly ground pepper

DIPPING SAUCE

1/2 cup plain yogurt

1/2 cup fruit chutney, finely chopped

1/2 teaspoon curry powder

1/4 cup dry white wine

1/4 teaspoon grated fresh ginger

❶ Heat oven to 375°F. Spray 13x9-inch pan with nonstick cooking spray.

❷ In food processor, finely chop shrimp, pork, celery, green onions and water chestnuts.

❸ In large bowl, combine eggs, soy sauce, bread crumbs, salt, pepper and meat mixture; mix well. Shape into 36 (1-inch) meatballs. Arrange meatballs 1 inch apart on pan. Bake 18 to 20 minutes or until browned and no longer pink in center. Drain; discard drippings.

❹ In large bowl, combine yogurt, chutney, curry powder, wine and ginger; mix well. Serve with meatballs.

12 servings.

Bruschetta, Canapés, Crostini & Sandwiches

CRABBIES

BETTY GRETCH
OWENDALE, MICHIGAN

1 (5-oz.) jar processed cheese spread
½ cup butter
1 tablespoon chopped onion
2 tablespoons salad dressing or mayonnaise
1 (6-oz.) pkg. lump crabmeat, drained, flaked
6 English muffins, split

❶ Heat oven to 350°F. Spray baking sheet with non-stick cooking spray.

❷ In medium saucepan, melt cheese and butter over medium heat. Add onion, dressing and crabmeat; mix well. Spoon mixture evenly onto English muffin halves; cut into quarters.

❸ Place English muffins on prepared sheet. Bake 12 to 15 minutes or until bubbly and light brown.

12 servings.

CRABMEAT HORS D'OEUVRES

EUGENE SHAFFER
OMAHA, NEBRASKA

1 (7-oz.) can lump crabmeat, drained, flaked
½ cup sour cream
1 tablespoon fresh lemon juice
2 tablespoons minced onion
½ teaspoon Worcestershire sauce
1 cup (4 oz.) shredded Swiss cheese
1 loaf cocktail rye bread

❶ Heat oven to 400°F.

❷ In large bowl, combine crabmeat, sour cream, lemon juice, onion, Worcestershire sauce and cheese; mix well. Place 1 teaspoonful of mixture on each bread slice. Arrange slices on baking sheet. Bake 10 minutes or until cheese is melted.

24 servings.

PARTY ROUND APPETIZERS

AUDREY DERR
VALRICO, FLORIDA

⅔ cup chopped onions
1 cup ripe olives, chopped
⅔ cup cooked crumbled bacon
2 cups (8 oz.) grated Swiss cheese
½ cup mayonnaise
2 teaspoons Worcestershire sauce
½ teaspoon salt, if desired
6 to 8 fresh mushrooms, chopped
1 loaf cocktail rye bread

❶ Heat oven to 350°F.

❷ In large bowl, combine onion, olives, bacon, cheese, mayonnaise, Worcestershire sauce, salt and mushrooms; mix well. Spread 1 to 2 tablespoons mixture evenly onto each bread slice. Place slices on baking sheet. Bake 15 minutes or until lightly browned.

24 servings.

FALAFEL

SHEILA SLOAN
HULL, GEORGIA

2 (15-oz.) cans garbanzo beans, rinsed, drained
1/2 cup grated onions
1/2 cup chopped fresh parsley
1 egg white
1 garlic clove, minced
1 teaspoon ground cumin
1/4 teaspoon salt
1/4 teaspoon freshly ground pepper
Dash of cayenne pepper
3 large whole-wheat pita breads, halved, heated
2 cups shredded leaf lettuce
3/4 cup hummus
Tomato slices, if desired

❶ In food processor, combine beans, onions, parsley, egg white, garlic, cumin, salt, pepper and cayenne; pulse until mixture resembles coarse cornmeal. Refrigerate, covered, 30 minutes. Shape mixture into thin 2-inch patties.

❷ Spray large skillet with nonstick cooking spray. Heat skillet over medium-high heat until hot. Cook patties 3 minutes on each side or until crispy and golden.

❸ Open pocket of each pita half. Line each pocket with lettuce. Place 2 or 3 patties in each pita. Spread patties with 2 tablespoons hummus. Serve with tomato slices.

6 servings.

HAM AND CRANBERRY SANDWICHES

LINDA DUNN
SPRINGDALE, ARKANSAS

1/2 cup whipped cream cheese
1/2 cup whole berry cranberry sauce
18 slices cinnamon bread, crusts removed
1 lb. thinly sliced ham

❶ In small bowl, combine cream cheese and cranberry sauce; mix well. Spread mixture evenly over each bread slice. Top 9 bread slices with 2 slices ham, then another bread slice. Place another 2 slices ham over top bread slice. Cut into 4 triangles.

18 servings.

QUICK CUKE CANAPES

DAVID HEPPNER
BRANDON, FLORIDA

2 medium cucumbers, refrigerated
1 (3-oz.) pkg. cream cheese, softened
2 tablespoons finely chopped fresh parsley
2 tablespoons finely chopped chives
1 tablespoon sour cream or mayonnaise
1 teaspoon prepared horseradish
1/2 teaspoon fresh lemon juice
1/2 cup shelled, deveined cooked shrimp, finely chopped

❶ Draw tines of fork lengthwise through cucumber peel to score; cut into 1/2-inch-thick slices. Drain on paper towels.

❷ In small bowl, combine cream cheese, parsley, chives, sour cream, horseradish and lemon juice; beat at medium speed until smooth. Stir in shrimp.

❸ Spread or pipe 1 teaspoon cream cheese mixture onto each cucumber slice.

12 servings.

GARLIC-MUSHROOM APPETIZER

CHRIS McBEE
XENIA, OHIO

1/2 cup vegetable or olive oil

1 cup chopped onions

3 tablespoons margarine

2 lb. fresh mushrooms, sliced

1 (28-oz.) can crushed tomatoes in puree, undrained

1 teaspoon salt

1 teaspoon freshly ground pepper

1/2 cup cider vinegar

1 1/2 cups chopped fresh parsley

3 garlic cloves, minced

Sliced French bread

❶ In large saucepan, heat oil over medium-high heat until hot. Add onions; sauté until transparent. Add mushrooms; cook 2 minutes. Reduce heat to medium. Add tomatoes, salt and pepper; simmer, covered, 20 to 30 minutes or until tomatoes are very tender. Stir in vinegar, parsley and garlic; simmer, covered, 10 minutes. Refrigerate several hours or overnight. To serve, spoon 2 tablespoons cold mixture evenly over each slice French bread.

12 to 16 servings.

REUBEN MINIATURES

CHRISANN LEWERT
EASTON, PENNSYLVANIA

6 slices rye or wheat bread, quartered

1 lb. sliced corn beef

1/2 cup Russian or Thousand Island dressing

1 (14-oz.) can sauerkraut, drained

1/2 lb. sliced Swiss or American cheese, each slice quartered

❶ Heat broiler. Arrange bread slices on broiler pan 4 to 6 inches from heat; toast until light brown and crisp.

❷ On each quarter, place about 5 slices corned beef and 1/4 cup sauerkraut. Pour 1 teaspoon dressing over sauerkraut; top with slice of cheese.

❸ Broil 4 to 6 inches from heat an additional 2 minutes or until cheese melts and begins to brown.

24 servings.

MINI MONTE CRISTO SANDWICHES

LUCY LIGHT
McCOOK, NEBRASKA

1/4 cup plus 2 tablespoons butter

2 tablespoons prepared mustard

8 slices white bread

4 oz. sliced Swiss cheese

4 oz. sliced ham

3 large eggs

1/2 cup milk

1 (1-oz.) pkg. dry onion soup mix

❶ In small bowl, combine 2 tablespoons butter and mustard; mix well. Spread mixture evenly over each bread slice. Divide cheese and ham evenly over 4 slices bread; top with remaining bread, buttered side down. Cut each sandwich into 4 triangles.

❷ In medium bowl, beat eggs, milk and onion soup mix at medium speed until well blended. Dip sandwiches in egg mixture, coating well.

❸ In large skillet, melt 1/4 cup butter over medium heat. Add sandwiches; cook about 4 minutes, turning once until golden.

8 servings.

CURRIED CHICKEN TEA SANDWICHES

DR. LYNNA AUSBURN
CLEVELAND, OKLAHOMA

1/2 cup chopped almonds

1/2 cup flaked coconut

1 (8-oz.) pkg. cream cheese, softened

1/4 teaspoon salt

1/4 teaspoon freshly ground pepper

1 1/2 teaspoons curry powder

2 tablespoons orange marmalade

2 cups diced cooked chicken

12 slices bread (1/2 inch thick)

3 tablespoons sliced green onions

❶ Heat oven to 350°F. Spray 3-quart casserole with nonstick cooking spray.

❷ Place almonds and coconut in casserole. Bake 5 to 10 minutes, stirring occasionally, until toasted and golden brown.

❸ In medium bowl, combine cream cheese, salt, pepper, curry powder and marmalade; mix well. Gently fold in chicken. Spread mixture evenly onto each bread slice. Trim crusts; cut each slice into 3 strips. Sprinkle evenly with coconut, almonds and green onions.

12 servings.

BRIOCHE EN SURPRISE

JOHN BITTER
MONTGOMERY, ALABAMA

1 loaf brioche, cut into 1/2-inch slices

3/4 cup mayonnaise

1 to 2 small red onions, sliced

3/4 cup chopped fresh parsley

❶ With 1 1/2-inch round cutter, cut 48 circles from bread. Spread mayonnaise evenly over each circle. Place onion slices on half of bread circles; top with remaining circles. Spread sandwiches in remaining mayonnaise, then roll in parsley. Refrigerate, covered, until ready to serve.

12 servings.

OLIVE-ONION CROSTINI

TAMARA BANDSTRA
GRAND HAVEN, MICHIGAN

1 cup ripe olives, pitted, drained, chopped

1/2 cup (2 oz.) freshly grated Parmesan cheese

1/2 cup mayonnaise

2 green onions, finely chopped

1/8 teaspoon salt

1/8 teaspoon freshly ground pepper

1 sourdough baguette, cut diagonally into 1/2-inch slices

❶ Heat broiler. Line broiler pan with aluminum foil.

❷ In medium bowl, combine olives, cheese, mayonnaise and onions; mix well. Season with salt and pepper.

❸ Mound 1 tablespoon olive mixture evenly over each bread slice. Arrange bread slices on prepared pan. Broil 4 to 6 inches from heat 2 minutes or until topping begins to brown. Serve hot.

12 servings.

SMOKED SALMON APPETIZERS

LINDA DUNN
SPRINGDALE, ARKANSAS

1 (3-oz.) pkg. cream cheese, softened
¼ cup sour cream
1 tablespoon honey
½ teaspoon freshly ground pepper
¼ teaspoon sea salt
48 slices cocktail bread, cut into 2-inch pieces
12 oz. smoked salmon
48 very thin slices cucumbers
¼ cup minced red onions
¼ cup chopped fresh dill

❶ In medium bowl, combine cream cheese, sour cream, honey, pepper and salt; mix well. Spread ½ teaspoon of the mixture evenly over each bread slice. Layer each slice with salmon and cucumber; sprinkle with onions. Garnish with dill.

24 servings.

COUNTRY CHEESE SNACKS

ELEANOR BERGERON
MESA, ARIZONA

1 cup mayonnaise
1 cup (4 oz.) grated fresh Parmesan cheese
1 (8-oz.) pkg. cream cheese, softened
2 green onions with tops, minced
1 loaf rye bread, sliced, each slice cut into 2-inch squares
Fresh parsley sprigs
½ cup stuffed green olives, sliced

❶ Heat broiler. Line broiler pan with aluminum foil.

❷ In small bowl, combine mayonnaise, Parmesan cheese, cream cheese and onions; mix well. Spread mixture evenly over each bread slice. Arrange bread slices on prepared pan. Broil 4 inches from heat 1 to 2 minutes or until golden and bubbly. Garnish with parsley and olives. Serve immediately.

24 servings.

BRUSCHETTA AND ROASTED GARLIC SPREAD

MARI YOUNKIN
COLORADO SPRINGS, COLORADO

2 garlic bulbs, tops removed
6 tablespoons extra-virgin olive oil
1 tablespoon seasoned pepper
1 (8-oz.) pkg. cream cheese, softened
¼ cup butter, softened
1 tablespoon chopped fresh Italian parsley
1 shallot, minced
⅓ cup plus 1 tablespoon chopped green onions
1 baguette, sliced, grilled
5 plum tomatoes, chopped
2 tablespoons chopped fresh basil
2 tablespoons chopped fresh oregano
1 tablespoon balsamic vinegar
1 cup (4 oz.) freshly grated Parmesan cheese

❶ Heat oven to 375°F. Line 3-quart casserole with aluminum foil. Place garlic, stem side down in casserole. Pour 3 tablespoons of the oil over garlic; sprinkle with pepper. Bake 25 minutes or until garlic is tender when pierced with knife. Turn oven off.

❷ Remove garlic from oven; cool slightly. Squeeze garlic cloves from each bulb onto flat plate. Using fork, mash cloves with olive oil and pepper into paste. Set aside.

❸ In food processor, combine cream cheese, butter, parsley, shallot and 1 tablespoon of the green onions; process until smooth. Stir in garlic mixture. Spread mixture evenly over baguette slices.

❹ In medium bowl, toss together tomatoes, remaining ⅓ cup green onions, remaining 3 tablespoons oil, basil, oregano and balsamic vinegar; mix well. Spoon mixture evenly onto baguette slices. Sprinkle with cheese. Serve immediately or broil 4 to 6 inches from heat 2 to 3 minutes or until cheese is slightly melted.

12 servings.

SHRIMP CANAPES WITH DILL

SHRIMP CANAPES WITH DILL

**SHEILA SLOAN
HULL, GEORGIA**

1/4 cup butter, softened

12 melba toast rounds

18 shelled, deveined medium cooked shrimp, halved lengthwise

1/4 cup mayonnaise

12 fresh dill sprigs

Freshly ground pepper

Lemon wedges

❶ Butter toast rounds. Arrange 3 shrimp pieces in spiral on each round. Using star tip on pastry bag, pipe mayonnaise stars on each round. Top with dill sprigs and pepper. Serve with lemon wedges.

6 servings.

ITALIAN SALSA

**NICOLE RIEGL
PHOENIXVILLE, PENNSYLVANIA**

6 tomatoes, chopped, drained

2 garlic cloves, chopped

1/4 cup chopped fresh basil

Dash of extra-virgin olive oil

Dash of balsamic vinegar

1/8 teaspoon salt

1/8 teaspoon freshly ground pepper

1 baguette, sliced

❶ In medium bowl, combine tomatoes, garlic, basil, oil and vinegar; mix well. Season with salt and pepper. Serve with baguette slices.

12 servings.

FRESH TOMATO BRUSCHETTA

**JANICE POGOZELSKI
CLEVELAND, OHIO**

1/2 cup extra-virgin olive oil

1 tablespoon garlic powder

1/8 teaspoon salt

1/8 teaspoon freshly ground pepper

1 baguette, cut diagonally into 1/2-inch slices

1 lb. vine-ripened tomatoes, diced

1 medium roasted red bell pepper, diced

1 bunch scallions (white parts only), grilled, chopped

3 garlic cloves, minced

1 Anaheim chile, roasted, minced

1 tablespoon balsamic vinegar

1 tablespoon chopped fresh basil

1 cup (4 oz.) freshly grated Parmesan cheese

❶ Heat oven to 375°F.

❷ In small bowl, combine olive oil, garlic powder, salt and pepper; mix well. Brush each bread slice evenly with oil mixture. Place slices on baking sheets. Bake 10 minutes or until toasted and brown. Remove from oven and cool.

❸ In large nonreactive bowl, combine tomatoes, bell pepper, scallions, garlic, chile pepper, vinegar and basil; mix well. Place 1 tablespoon tomato mixture evenly onto each bread slice. Sprinkle with cheese. Warm slightly in microwave before serving.

15 servings.

SPIDINI

SANDRA THOMPSON
WHITE HALL, ARKANSAS

½ cup butter

2 tablespoons minced onion

2 tablespoons poppy seeds

1½ tablespoons prepared mustard

1 loaf French bread, sliced lengthwise

6 thick slices bacon, cooked, crumbled

1 cup (4 oz.) shredded. mozzarella cheese

❶ Heat oven to 350°F.

❷ In small saucepan, melt butter over medium heat. Add onion; cook 2 minutes or until onion is tender. Stir in poppy seeds and mustard; mix well. Brush onion mixture evenly onto cut surfaces of French bread.

❸ Sprinkle half the crumbled bacon on bottom half of sliced loaf; top with cheese, then remaining bacon. Top with remaining half sliced bread; wrap in aluminum foil. Bake 15 to 20 minutes or until cheese is melted. Slice into 1-inch slices.

8 servings.

MUSHROOM SALSA

NICOLE RIEGL
PHOENIXVILLE, PENNSYLVANIA

2 tablespoons olive oil

2 lb. mixed fresh mushrooms (portobello, brown and shittake, etc.), chopped

3 garlic cloves, chopped

2 tablespoons white wine

2 tablespoons chopped fresh rosemary

1 tablespoon balsamic vinegar

⅛ teaspoon salt

⅛ teaspoon freshly ground pepper

❶ In large skillet, heat oil over medium-high heat until hot. Add mushrooms and garlic; sauté 4 to 6 minutes or until mushrooms are tender. Stir in wine, rosemary and vinegar. Season with salt and pepper. Serve at room temperature.

12 servings.

CUCUMBER SANDWICHES

VIVIAN NIKANOW
CHICAGO, ILLINOIS

1 (8-oz.) pkg. cream cheese, softened

1 (.7-oz.) envelope Italian dressing mix

1 loaf cocktail rye bread

2 cucumbers, sliced

2 teaspoons paprika

❶ In small bowl, combine cream cheese and dressing mix; mix well. Spread cheese mixture evenly over each slice of bread; top each with cucumber slice. Sprinkle with paprika.

24 servings.

SUMMER CROSTINI

MICHELLE JONES
BLOOMFIELD HILLS, MICHIGAN

1 cup (4 oz.) goat cheese

12 (¼-inch) baguette slices, toasted

12 slices arugula

2 roasted red bell peppers, sliced

❶ Spread goat cheese evenly over each toasted round. Top each with 1 slice arugula and bell pepper slices.

6 servings.

MUSHROOMS ON CRISPY TOAST

GWEN CAMPBELL
STERLING, VIRGINIA

1 lb. chanterelle mushrooms

1 tablespoon melted butter

2 tablespoons butter

1 small green onion (white part only), finely chopped

⅛ teaspoon salt

1 tablespoon fresh or dried thyme

2 tablespoons butter

4 slices white or wheat bread

3 tablespoons sour cream

1 green onion (green part only), finely slivered

❶ Lightly brush mushrooms with 1 tablespoon melted butter. Chop mushrooms.

❷ In large skillet, melt 1 tablespoon of the butter over medium heat. Add green onions and mushrooms; sauté until onions are tender and mushroom liquid has evaporated. Sprinkle with salt and thyme. Remove from skillet.

❸ Add remaining 1 tablespoon butter to skillet. Add bread slices; cook until brown and crisp. Remove bread from skillet. Cut each bread slice into quarters; arrange on large platter. Scatter chopped mushroom pieces evenly over bread; top with dollop of sour cream. Garnish with green onions.

8 servings.

HAM AND SWISS CANAPES

LANNIE EISENBRANDT
MAHTOMEDI, MINNESOTA

1½ cups grated Swiss cheese

½ cup mayonnaise

Dash of hot pepper sauce

4 teaspoons prepared mustard

4 slices boiled ham

1 kosher dill pickle, quartered lengthwise

❶ In small bowl, combine cheese, mayonnaise, pepper sauce and mustard; mix well. Spread each ham slice evenly with one-fourth of the cheese mixture. Place pickle slice across short end of ham slice; roll up. Refrigerate. Cut into bite-size pieces before serving.

4 servings.

RYE SWISS OF COURSE

VICKI HOSS
SAN CARLOS, CALIFORNIA

4 cups (1 lb.) grated Swiss cheese

1 tablespoon Worcestershire sauce

1 teaspoon garlic powder

1 (2-oz.) jar pimientos, drained, diced

2 green onions, sliced

1 loaf cocktail rye bread, sliced

❶ Heat broiler.

❷ In medium bowl, combine cheese, Worcestershire sauce, garlic powder, pimientos and onions; mix well. Spread mixture evenly over each bread slice. Arrange bread slices on broiler pan.

❸ Broil 4 to 6 inches from heat 2 minutes or until bubbly. Serve immediately.

24 servings.

BACON QUICKIES

ANN NACE
PERKASIE, PENNSYLVANIA

1 (10.5-oz.) can condensed cream of mushroom soup

24 slices bread, crusts removed

24 thick slices bacon, cut into thirds

❶ Spread soup over bread slices. Cut each slice into thirds. Roll slices, starting at short edge, jelly roll style.

❷ Wrap 1 piece bacon around each bread roll; secure with toothpick. Arrange on broiler pan.

❸ Heat broiler. Broil 4 to 6 inches from heat about 3 minutes, turning once, until bacon is crisp.

24 servings.

BRUSCHETTA

DEANNA JONES
PARKER, COLORADO

½ cup salad dressing or mayonnaise

1 cup (4 oz.) shredded mozzarella cheese

2 medium tomatoes, halved, seeded, finely diced

¼ cup chopped pitted ripe olives

¼ cup (1 oz.) grated fresh Parmesan cheese

1 teaspoon chopped fresh oregano

½ teaspoon freshly ground pepper

¼ teaspoon basil

⅓ cup butter, softened

1 baguette, cut into 1-inch slices

❶ Heat oven to 350°F.

❷ In large bowl, combine salad dressing, mozzarella, tomatoes, olives, Parmesan, oregano, pepper and basil; mix well.

❸ Butter 1 side of each bread slice. Arrange slices, buttered side up, on baking sheet. Divide and spread tomato mixture evenly over each slice. Bake 15 minutes or until hot and cheese is melted. Serve warm.

12 servings.

ROASTED RED PEPPER BRUSCHETTA

ALICE CHARLTON
MARATHON, FLORIDA

1 loaf Italian bread, cut into ½-inch slices

1 (7.25-oz.) jar roasted red peppers, drained, rinsed, chopped

¼ cup chopped red onions

¼ teaspoon salt

⅓ cup loosely packed arugula, chopped

1 tablespoon chopped fresh basil

2 teaspoons balsamic vinegar

1 garlic clove, minced

¼ teaspoon sugar

¼ teaspoon freshly ground pepper

❶ Heat broiler. Line broiler pan with aluminum foil.

❷ Arrange bread slices in single layer on prepared pan. Broil 4 to 6 inches from heat, 1 to 2 minutes or until lightly browned, turning once.

❸ In medium bowl, combine red peppers, onions, salt, arugula, basil, vinegar, garlic, sugar and pepper; mix well. Divide mixture evenly over each bread slice.

24 appetizers.

ROASTED RED PEPPER BRUSCHETTA

CHEESE LOAF

SANDRA THOMPSON
WHITE HALL, ARKANSAS

1 loaf French bread

2 tablespoons butter, melted

2 eggs

1 (8-oz.) pkg. cream cheese, softened

¾ cup reduced-fat milk

¼ cup all-purpose flour

½ teaspoon chili powder

¼ teaspoon salt

½ cup (2 oz.) shredded cheddar cheese

1 (4-oz.) can chopped mild green chiles, if desired, drained

❶ Heat oven to 350°F.

❷ Cut 1-inch layer off top of bread; discard. Scoop inside out, leaving ½-inch-thick bread shell. Tear soft bread into 1-inch pieces. Brush shell with butter; wrap in aluminum foil. Bake 7 to 9 minutes or until shell is hot and crisp.

❸ In food processor, combine eggs, cream cheese, ½ cup milk, flour, chili powder and salt; blend until smooth.

❹ Place hot crust on baking sheet; pour egg mixture into crust. Add remaining ¼ cup milk; stir with fork. Push enough of the chunks of reserved bread into shell to bring filling to top of crust; wrap in foil. Bake 45 minutes or until filling is set. Remove from oven; sprinkle with cheese and chiles. Cool 15 minutes. Slice into 1-inch slices.

8 servings.

HOT ASPARAGUS CANAPES

MARY HARDT
BETHESDA, MARYLAND

20 thin slices bread, crusts removed

2 tablespoons blue cheese

1 (8-oz.) pkg. cream cheese, softened

20 asparagus spears, cooked

¼ cup butter, melted

❶ Flatten bread slices with rolling pin. In medium bowl, combine blue cheese and cream cheese until well blended. Spread cheese mixture evenly over each bread slice. Place asparagus spear on edge of bread slice; roll up tightly. Secure with toothpick.

❷ Heat oven to 400°F.

❸ Brush each roll with butter. Arrange rolls on baking pan. Bake 15 minutes or until lightly browned. Cut each into thirds.

20 servings.

CREAM CHEESE BRUSCHETTA

MARY ANNE HART
KENMORE, NEW YORK

¼ cup olive oil

1 garlic clove, minced

1 (1-lb.) loaf French bread, cut lengthwise

1 (8-oz.) pkg. cream cheese, softened

3 tablespoons grated Parmesan cheese

1 (2¼-oz.) can sliced ripe olives, drained

1 cup chopped plum tomatoes

Chopped fresh basil

❶ Heat oven to 400°F.

❷ In small bowl, combine oil and garlic; mix well. Spread oil mixture evenly over cut side of bread. Arrange bread slices on baking sheet. Bake 10 to 12 minutes or until bread begins to brown; cool.

❸ In medium bowl, combine cream cheese and Parmesan; beat at medium speed until well mixed. Spread cream cheese mixture evenly over bottom half of bread. Top with olives, tomatoes and basil. Sprinkle with additional Parmesan cheese, if desired. Cut bread into diagonal pieces.

12 servings.

HOT ASPARAGUS CANAPES

SMOKED SALMON COCKTAIL BITES

CARLYN LINSLEY
PITTSBURGH, PENNSYLVANIA

SALMON FILLING
1/2 (8-oz.) pkg. cream cheese, softened
3 oz. smoked salmon, chopped
1 tablespoon whipping cream
2 teaspoons fresh lemon juice
1/8 teaspoon freshly ground pepper

WATERCRESS FILLING
1 cup firmly packed watercress leaves
1/3 cup mayonnaise
1 oz. cream cheese, softened

CRUST
15 slices very thinly sliced whole wheat bread
10 slices very thinly sliced white bread
1/4 cup butter, softened

❶ In food processor, combine 4 oz. cream cheese, salmon, cream, lemon juice and pepper; process until well combined. Transfer cheese mixture to medium bowl. Wash and dry food processor bowl. Add watercress, mayonnaise and 1 oz. cream cheese; process until well combined.

❷ Lightly spread one side of all bread slices with butter. Spread 1 generous tablespoon of the cheese mixture evenly onto each of 10 slices whole wheat bread. Spread 1 tablespoon of the watercress filling evenly onto each of 10 slices white bread. Stack 1 salmon and 1 watercress slice; top with 1 whole wheat slice, buttered side down. Repeat the process, making 5 sandwich stacks.

❸ Wrap sandwiches in aluminum foil; arrange on serving platter. Place second serving platter on top to weight lightly. Refrigerate 1 hour or up to 24 hours. Unwrap sandwiches and trim crusts. Slice into 1/2-inch strips.

20 servings.

CHEESE PUFF SOUFFLES

KIMBERLY RAY
HOUSTON, TEXAS

1 (20-oz.) jar processed cheddar cheese spread, softened
1 lb. butter, softened
1 teaspoon hot pepper sauce
1 teaspoon onion powder
1 1/2 teaspoons Worcestershire sauce
Pinch cayenne pepper
2 tablespoons dill weed
3 loaves thin-sliced bread, crusts removed

❶ Heat oven to 325°F. Line baking sheet with parchment paper.

❷ In large bowl, beat cheese and butter at medium speed until smooth. Add pepper sauce, onion powder, Worcestershire sauce, cayenne and dill weed; mix well.

❸ Spread half of cheese mixture evenly over each bread slice. Stack slices using 3 slices per sandwich. Cut each sandwich into 6 pieces.

❹ Bake 15 minutes or until edges brown.

28 servings.

CAVIAR AND EGG CANAPES

**ROBERT HADAN
WARREN, MICHIGAN**

5 hard-cooked extra-large eggs, peeled
Unsalted butter, softened
1 loaf deli pumpernickel bread, cut into 30 (2-inch) squares
6 oz. black caviar

❶ Using an egg slicer, slice eggs. Separate yolks from egg white rings; set rings aside. Finely chop remaining egg whites (not rings); add to yolks. Using fingers, press yolks and chopped whites through strainer to fluff.

❷ Butter bread slices. Place egg white ring on each slice. Place dollop of caviar in center of each ring. Sprinkle with fluffed egg.

30 servings.

BACON AND CHEESE TOASTIES

**TANYA DEFRANCES
PITTSBURGH, PENNSYLVANIA**

1 (1-lb.) pkg. thick-sliced bacon, cooked, crumbled
1 medium onion, finely chopped
2 cups (8 oz.) shredded cheddar cheese
1 cup mayonnaise
1 baguette, cut into ¼-inch slices

❶ Heat broiler.

❷ In medium bowl, combine bacon, onion and cheese; mix well. Add enough mayonnaise to make mixture of spreading consistency. Spread bacon mixture evenly over each bread slice. Arrange bread slices on broiler pan.

❸ Broil 4 to 6 inches from heat 2 minutes or until bubbly. Serve immediately.

20 servings.

PUMPERNICKEL PORKIES

**BRENDA HENDRIKX
ST. CLOUD, MINNESOTA**

1 lb. bulk Italian pork sausage
1 lb. ground beef
1 lb. processed cheese spread loaf, cut into ½-inch cubes
1 teaspoon oregano
½ teaspoon Italian seasoning
¼ teaspoon freshly ground pepper
1 loaf cocktail rye bread, sliced

❶ In large skillet, cook sausage and beef over medium heat, crumbling into small pieces, until brown. Drain fat; return to heat. Add cheese, oregano, Italian seasoning and pepper. Stir over low heat until cheese is melted. Spread 1½ tablespoons sausage mixture evenly over each bread slice.

❷ Heat broiler. Arrange bread slices on baking sheet. Broil 4 to 6 inches from heat 2 minutes or until cheese is lightly browned. Transfer to serving platter. Serve warm.

24 servings.

Dips
&
Salsas

CHILI DIP

ROSE DEVITO
LONG BRANCH, NEW JERSEY

1 (8-oz.) pkg. cream cheese
1 (16-oz.) can chili (with or without beans)
1 cup (4 oz.) taco-flavored shredded cheese

❶ Place cream cheese in glass microwaveable 9-inch pie plate. Pour chili over cream cheese; top with shredded cheese. Microwave 5 minutes at High power or until cheese is melted. Serve with your favorite chips or crackers, if desired.

12 servings.

MEXICAN DIP

LINDA LOUGHLIN
WORCESTER, MASSACHUSETTS

1 lb. ground beef
1 (1¼-oz.) pkg. taco seasoning mix
1 (16-oz.) can refried beans
2 (8-oz.) pkg. cream cheese, softened
1 (16-oz.) jar salsa
2 cups (8 oz.) shredded taco-flavored cheese

❶ Heat oven to 350°F.

❷ In large skillet, sauté beef over medium-high heat until no longer pink in center. Drain; add taco seasoning mix. Stir in refried beans.

❸ In medium bowl, combine cream cheese and salsa. Spread mixture into 1½-quart casserole. Layer meat mixture evenly over cream cheese mixture. Top with cheese. Bake 15 to 20 or until cheese melts. Serve with taco chips, if desired.

12 servings.

FRUIT DIP

DELIA KENNEDY
DEER PARK, WASHINGTON

1 (8-oz.) pkg. cream cheese, softened
¼ cup shredded coconut
¼ cup sugar
¼ cup fresh lime juice
¼ cup sherry

❶ In blender, combine cream cheese, coconut, sugar, lime juice and sherry; blend until smooth. Refrigerate, covered, until ready to serve. Serve with fresh fruit, if desired.

8 servings.

"GET TOGETHER" ROASTED PEPPER AND ARTICHOKE DIP

GWEN CAMPBELL
STERLING, VIRGINIA

1 (14-oz.) can artichoke hearts, drained, coarsely chopped
1 cup chopped roasted red bell peppers
¼ cup green onions, chopped (white parts only)
½ cup mayonnaise
½ cup sour cream
1 teaspoon Worcestershire sauce
2 teaspoons dry sherry
1 cup (4 oz.) grated mozzarella cheese
1 cup (4 oz.) freshly grated Parmesan cheese
1 teaspoon cayenne pepper
1 cup chopped fresh Italian parsley

❶ In large bowl, combine artichoke hearts, bell peppers, onions, mayonnaise, sour cream, Worcestershire sauce, sherry, cheeses, cayenne and parsley; mix well. Refrigerate, covered, 30 minutes.

❷ Heat oven to 350°F. Stir mixture; transfer to 1½-quart casserole. Bake 15 to 20 minutes or until lightly browned and heated through. Serve with crackers or fresh vegetables, if desired.

12 servings.

PEANUT DIP

JANICE POGOZELSKI
CLEVELAND, OHIO

1 cup smooth peanut butter

2 tablespoons low-sodium soy sauce

1 tablespoon fresh lime juice

1 tablespoon vegetable oil

1 1/2 tablespoons honey

1 teaspoon crushed red pepper

1 garlic clove, pressed

1/2 teaspoon hot pepper sauce

❶ In medium bowl, combine peanut butter, soy sauce, lime juice, oil, honey, red pepper, garlic and hot pepper sauce; mix well. Refrigerate, covered, until ready to use. Serve with vegetable sticks, if desired.

6 servings.

SALSA DIP

JENI SANDHEINRICH
SAINT LIBORY, ILLINOIS

1 (8-oz.) pkg. cream cheese, softened

8 oz. sour cream

1 (1 1/4-oz.) pkg. taco seasoning mix

10 (10-inch) flour tortillas

Salsa

❶ In medium bowl, combine cream cheese, sour cream and taco seasoning; mix well. Spread mixture evenly over 5 of the tortillas. Cover each of the 5 tortillas with second tortilla. Spread cream cheese mixture evenly over each tortilla. Continue to alternate layers until all tortillas are used. Cut stack into wedges. Serve with salsa.

12 servings.

REUBEN DIP

DELIA KENNEDY
DEER PARK, WASHINGTON

1 1/2 cups (6 oz.) shredded Swiss cheese

1/2 cup sauerkraut

1 cup Thousand Island dressing

2 (2.5-oz.) pkg. dried corn beef

❶ Heat oven to 350°F. Spray 13x9-inch pan with nonstick cooking spray.

❷ In large bowl, combine cheese, sauerkraut, dressing and corn beef; mix well. Spread mixture into bottom of pan. Bake 20 minutes or until hot and bubbling. Serve with rye chips.

12 servings.

HUMMUS A LA CHARLOTTE

CHARLOTTE WARD
HILTON HEAD ISLAND, SOUTH CAROLINA

2 garlic cloves, finely minced

1 (19-oz.) can chickpeas, rinsed, drained

1/2 cup fresh lemon juice

2 tablespoons chopped fresh parsley

3 tablespoons olive oil

1 tablespoon lemon pepper

1 teaspoon dried dill weed

6 teaspoons freshly grated lemon peel

❶ In food processor, puree garlic and chickpeas. Add lemon juice, parsley, oil, lemon pepper, dill weed and lemon peel; process until smooth and well blended. Transfer hummus to serving bowl. Serve with pita bread, vegetables or tortilla chips, if desired.

8 servings.

COCONUT FRUIT DIP

PAMELA THOMPSON
IPSWICH, MASSACHUSETTS

1 (8-oz.) can crushed unsweetened pineapple, undrained

¾ cup skim milk

½ cup reduced-fat sour cream

1 (3.4-oz.) pkg. instant coconut crème pudding mix

Fresh pineapple, grapes and strawberries

❶ In blender, combine pineapple, milk, sour cream and pudding mix; cover and blend on medium speed 1 minute or until smooth. Serve with fruit. Store in refrigerator.

12 servings.

FRESH SALSA

CHRIS McBEE
XENIA, OHIO

6 Anaheim chiles, roasted, diced

4 large tomatoes, chopped

3 green onions, sliced

2 tablespoons minced fresh cilantro

½ to 1 jalapeño chile, seeded, minced

1 garlic clove, minced

1 teaspoon vinegar

⅓ cup olive oil

½ teaspoon freshly ground pepper

1 teaspoon salt

❶ In medium bowl, combine chiles, tomatoes, onions, cilantro, chile and garlic. In a second bowl combine vinegar, oil, pepper and salt; stir into vegetable mixture. Cover and refrigerate 2 hours. Serve with tortilla chips.

12 servings.

JALAPENO CHEESE DIP

CAROL HAWLEY
FREDERICK, MARYLAND

4 cups (1 lb.) grated sharp cheddar cheese

1 medium onion, chopped

6 to 7 medium jalapeño chiles, chopped

2 cups mayonnaise or salad dressing

❶ In blender, combine cheese, onion, chiles and mayonnaise; blend until smooth. For spicier dip, add juices from chiles. Serve with tortilla chips, if desired.

12 servings.

BLT DIP

DELIA KENNEDY
DEER PARK, WASHINGTON

1 cup sour cream

1 lb. thick-sliced bacon, cooked, crumbled

1 cup mayonnaise

1 large tomato, chopped

❶ In large bowl, gently combine sour cream, bacon, mayonnaise and tomato; mix well. Refrigerate, covered, 1 hour or until chilled. Serve with toast pieces.

12 servings.

HOT CHILE AND CHEESE DIP

DEANNA JONES
PARKER, COLORADO

1 cup mayonnaise

½ cup (2-oz.) freshly grated Parmesan cheese

1 cup (4 oz.) shredded Monterey Jack cheese

3 (4-oz.) cans chopped green chiles, drained

1 (12-oz.) can whole kernel corn with diced red and green bell peppers, drained

2 tablespoons sliced ripe olives

❶ Heat oven to 325°F. Spray 2-quart casserole with nonstick cooking spray.

❷ In medium bowl, combine mayonnaise, cheeses, chiles and corn; stir until well blended. Spoon mixture into casserole.

❸ Bake 25 to 30 minutes or until thoroughly heated. Garnish with olives. Serve immediately.

12 servings.

FRUIT DIP

BARBARA BRANDEL
LAKELAND, FLORIDA

1 (8-oz.) pkg. cream cheese, softened

1 (7-oz.) jar marshmallow creme

1 tablespoon Triple Sec liqueur or cherry syrup

❶ In blender, combine cream cheese, marshmallow creme and liqueur; blend until smooth. Pour mixture into serving dish. Refrigerate, covered, until ready to serve.

10 servings.

CORN RELISH DIP

NORMA EDLEMON
DAVENPORT, IOWA

1 (16-oz.) jar corn relish, drained

2 cups sour cream

❶ In medium bowl, combine corn relish and sour cream; mix well. Remove mixture to serving bowl. Serve with crackers or fresh vegetables, if desired.

20 servings.

BLACK BEAN HUMMUS

TAMI ZYLKA
BLUE BELL, PENNSYLVANIA

1 (16-oz.) can black beans, drained, rinsed

½ cup salsa

2 tablespoons fresh lime juice

2 tablespoons chopped fresh cilantro

¼ teaspoon cumin

⅛ teaspoon salt

⅛ teaspoon freshly ground pepper

❶ In food processor, combine beans, salsa, lime juice, cilantro, cumin, salt and pepper; process until smooth. Transfer bean mixture to serving bowl. Serve with nacho chips or pita bread, if desired.

8 servings.

CHEESE AND HERB DIP

ERIN MITCHELL
STONE MOUNTAIN, GEORGIA

2/3 cup whipping cream

1 1/2 cups cream cheese, softened

2 tablespoons chopped fresh parsley

2 tablespoons chopped chives

2 tablespoons chopped fresh mint

2 finely chopped green onions

1 garlic clove, crushed

1 teaspoon fresh lemon juice

1/8 teaspoon salt

1/8 teaspoon freshly ground pepper

❶ In medium bowl, combine cream and cheese; mix well. Mixture should be light, but stiff enough to hold its shape. Add parsley, chives, mint, onions, garlic and lemon juice; mix well. Season with salt and pepper. Serve with vegetables.

12 servings.

SPICE-BUTTER HUMMUS

STEPHANIE KONTOS
BLOOMINGTON, MINNESOTA

3 garlic cloves, finely minced

1 (15-oz.) can butter beans, drained, 1/8 juice reserved

1/8 cup plus 2 tablespoons tahini

1/8 cup fresh lemon juice

1/4 teaspoon cayenne pepper

❶ In food processor, combine garlic, beans, reserved bean juice, tahini, lemon juice, and cayenne pepper; process until smooth. Transfer garlic mixture to serving bowl. Serve with pitas, crackers or chips, or spread on bagels in place of cream cheese, if desired.

8 servings.

PINA COLADA DIP

I.W. DAILEY
IRMO, SOUTH CAROLINA

1 1/2 cups cream cheese

3/4 cup piña colada mix

1/2 cup sour cream

1 1/4 cups pineapple chunks

1/2 cup maraschino cherries, halved

❶ In blender or food processor, combine cream cheese, piña colada mix and sour cream; blend until smooth. Transfer mixture to large bowl; fold in pineapple chunks and cherries. Refrigerate, covered, 1 hour. Serve with other fresh fruits or dried fruit.

24 servings.

TACO DIP

GERALD ROEDER
MOCKSVILLE, NORTH CAROLINA

12 oz. cream cheese, softened

1/2 cup sour cream

2 teaspoons chili powder

1 1/2 teaspoons ground cumin

1/8 teaspoon ground red pepper

1/2 cup salsa

2 cups shredded lettuce

1 cup (4 oz.) shredded cheddar cheese

1 cup (4 oz.) shredded Monterey Jack cheese

1/2 cup diced plum tomatoes

1/3 cup sliced green onions

1/4 cup sliced ripe olives

1/4 cup pimiento-stuffed green olives

❶ In large bowl, combine cream cheese, sour cream, chili powder, cumin and red pepper; mix until well blended. Stir in salsa. Spread mixture evenly into 10-inch serving platter lined with lettuce. Top with cheeses, tomatoes, green onions and olives. Serve with tortilla chips, if desired.

10 servings.

GAZPACHO DIP OR SOUP

JUDY RICHMOND
GORHAM, MAINE

1 (28-oz.) can chopped tomatoes

1 (15-oz.) can small tomato sauce

1 bunch green onions, chopped

1 (4.25-oz) can ripe olives, chopped

1 (4-oz.) can green chiles, chopped

2 tablespoons vinegar

2 tablespoons vegetable oil

1 tablespoon garlic salt

2 cucumbers, thinly sliced

❶ In large bowl, combine tomatoes, tomato sauce, green onions, olives, chiles, vinegar, oil, salt and cucumbers; mix well. Refrigerate, covered, 8 to 12 hours. Serve with tortilla chips, if desired.

10 servings.

BLACK BEAN SALSA

MICHELLE MORRILL
PRESCOTT VALLEY, ARIZONA

2 tomatoes, seeded, chopped

¼ cup chopped green onions with tops

2 tablespoons chopped fresh cilantro

1 jalapeño chile, seeded, finely chopped

2 garlic cloves, pressed

2 tablespoons fresh lime juice

1 (15-oz.) can black beans, rinsed, drained

¼ teaspoon salt

¼ teaspoon freshly ground pepper

❶ In medium bowl combine tomatoes, green onions, cilantro, chile, garlic, lime juice, beans, salt and pepper; mix well. Refrigerate, covered, 2 hours. Serve with tortilla chips or over warm cornbread, if desired.

12 servings.

COOL CUCUMBER SALSA

CHRIS McBEE
XENIA, OHIO

1 teaspoon salt

4 large cucumbers, seeded, finely diced

2 tablespoons fresh lemon juice

6 medium tomatoes, finely diced

1 medium red onion, finely diced

1 tablespoon chopped fresh cilantro

1 jalapeño chile, chopped

❶ In large bowl, combine salt, cucumbers, lemon juice, tomatoes, onion, cilantro and chile; mix well. Refrigerate, covered, 1 hour. Serve with chips, if desired.

12 servings.

ARTICHOKE AND CAPER DIP

NICOLE RIEGL
PHOENIXVILLE, PENNSYLVANIA

1 garlic clove

2 (7-oz.) cans artichoke hearts, packed in water, drained

1 (3-oz.) jar capers, drained

3 tablespoons fresh lemon juice

3 teaspoons freshly grated lemon peel

8 to 10 fresh basil leaves

1/2 cup extra virgin olive oil

1/8 teaspoon salt

1/8 teaspoon freshly ground pepper

❶ In food processor, chop garlic. Add artichoke hearts, capers, lemon juice, lemon peel and basil; chop until just mixed. With motor running, add thin stream of oil until mixture is smooth. Season with salt and pepper. Serve with baguette slices, flavored dried toast or bagel crackers, if desired.

12 servings.

GALLAGHER "CHOW-CHOW" (CHUNKY FRESH SALSA)

KIMBERLEY GALLAGHER
MOUNTLAKE TERRACE, WASHINGTON

1 (16-oz.) can black beans, rinsed, drained

1 (16-oz.) can whole-kernel corn, drained

1 small red onion, finely chopped

6 plum tomatoes, seeded, finely chopped

1/4 cup finely chopped fresh cilantro

1 tablespoon fresh lime juice

1 1/2 tablespoons fresh lemon juice

4 tablespoons finely chopped jalapeño chile

❶ In large bowl, combine beans, corn, onion, tomatoes, cilantro, lime juice, lemon juice and chile; mix well. Refrigerate, covered, up to 1 day before serving. Serve with tortilla chips, if desired.

12 servings.

APPLE-TOFFEE DIP

DIANE CARON
WINTERSET, IOWA

1 (8-oz.) pkg. cream cheese, softened

1/2 cup packed brown sugar

1/4 cup sugar

1 teaspoon vanilla extract

3 (9-oz.) toffee candy bars, chopped into 1/4-inch pieces

3 medium tart apples, cut into wedges

❶ In large bowl, beat cream cheese, sugars and vanilla at medium speed until well blended. Fold in toffee bars. Serve with apples. Store in refrigerator.

10 servings.

KATE'S GUACAMOLE

KATELYNN WILCHER
MOORESVILLE, INDIANA

3 to 4 firm ripe avocados, seeded, cut up

1 tablespoon fresh lime juice

3 garlic cloves, minced

3 tablespoons salsa

1/2 teaspoon chili powder

2 tablespoons sour cream

❶ In medium bowl, sprinkle avocado pieces with lime juice. Using potato masher, mash avocado. Stir in garlic, salsa, chili powder and sour cream; mix well. Refrigerate mixture, overnight or until ready to serve. Serve with tortilla chips, if desired.

6 servings.

TEX BEAN DIP

SARAH ROARK
ROSSVILLE, ILLINOIS

2 (16-oz.) cans refried beans

3 avocados, seeded

2 tablespoons fresh lemon juice

½ teaspoon salt

¼ teaspoon freshly ground pepper

1 cup sour cream

½ cup mayonnaise

1 (1¼-oz.) pkg. taco seasoning mix

2 cups (8 oz.) shredded cheddar cheese

1 cup pitted sliced ripe olives

4 green onions, sliced

1 large tomato, chopped

❶ Spread refried beans evenly onto 12-inch serving plate. In medium bowl, mash avocados with lemon juice, salt and pepper. Spread mixture evenly over beans.

❷ In small bowl, combine sour cream, mayonnaise and taco seasoning; mix well. Spread mixture evenly over avocado layer. Sprinkle with cheese, olives, onions and tomato. Serve with tortilla chips, if desired.

8 to 10 servings.

CHOCOLATE FRUIT DIP

GERALDINE REEP
LINCOLNTON, NORTH CAROLINA

6 oz. semisweet chocolate, melted

1 (14-oz.) can sweetened condensed milk

¼ cup milk

❶ In large bowl, combine chocolate and sweetened condensed milk; stir until smooth. Add milk; stir until blended. Serve with fruit, if desired.

10 servings.

ISLANDER CHEESE SPREAD

SAMANTHA CARROLL
ADENA, OHIO

2 (8-oz.) pkg. cream cheese, softened

1 (8-oz.) can crushed pineapple, drained

2 tablespoons chopped green onions, including tops

½ cup chopped green bell peppers

2 teaspoons seasoned salt

2 cups chopped pecans

❶ In medium bowl, beat cream cheese and pineapple at low speed until smooth. Add green onions, bell peppers, salt and pecans (reserving 1 tablespoon pecans). Remove mixture to serving bowl. Sprinkle remaining pecans over top. Serve with wheat or bacon-flavored crackers, if desired.

24 servings.

GREEN CHUTNEY

MADHULIKA KAPUR
HILLSIDE, ILLINOIS

1½ cups chopped fresh mint

1½ cups chopped fresh cilantro

1 bunch fresh cilantro

1 medium onion, chopped

1 to 3 jalapeño chiles, seeds removed, chopped

3 tablespoons fresh lemon juice

¼ teaspoon salt

❶ In blender, puree mint, cilantro, onion and chile. Pour mint mixture into jar with tight-fitting lid. Add lemon juice and salt. Cover jar; shake to blend. Serve with kabobs or grilled meat. Store in refrigerator.

8 servings.

TASTY CAVIAR

SHAMSA PIRANI
ATLANTA, GEORGIA

1 (15-oz.) can black-eyed peas, rinsed, drained

½ cup chopped red onions

½ cup chopped green bell peppers

2 jalapeño chiles, seeded, chopped

1 (2-oz.) jar minced pimientos, drained

2 garlic cloves, minced

1 tablespoon vegetable oil

½ cup zesty Italian dressing

Crackers or tortilla chips

❶ In large bowl, combine black-eyed peas, purple onions, bell peppers, chiles, pimientos, garlic, oil and dressing; mix well. Refrigerate, covered, overnight. Transfer mixture to serving dish. Serve with crackers or tortilla chips.

10 servings.

DILL DIP

SANDRA HOUNSOM
ST. LOUIS, MISSOURI

1 cup sour cream

1 cup mayonnaise

1½ tablespoons finely chopped onion

1½ teaspoons chopped fresh parsley

2 teaspoons dill weed

1½ teaspoons dill pickle juice

½ teaspoon celery seed

1½ teaspoons seasoned salt

❶ In large bowl, combine sour cream, mayonnaise, onion, parsley, dill, pickle juice, celery seed and salt; mix well. Refrigerate, covered, at least 8 hours before serving. Serve with chips, if desired.

10 servings.

TURKISH EGGPLANT DIP WITH YOGURT DRESSING

ALI MANGUOGLU
SALINA, KANSAS

1 large eggplant

1 green bell pepper

2 tablespoons fresh lemon juice

8 oz. plain yogurt

2 teaspoons salt

4 tablespoons olive oil

4 garlic cloves, crushed

4 pita breads, cut into small pieces

❶ Heat grill. Place eggplant and bell pepper on gas grill over medium heat or on charcoal grill 4 to 6 inches from medium coals. Cook 8 to 10 minutes, turning occasionally, until tender. Remove from grill; cool. Peel eggplant; discard seeds. Chop eggplant into small pieces; place in blender. Add lemon juice, yogurt, 1 teaspoon of the salt and olive oil to blender; blend until smooth.

❷ Cut bell pepper in half; discard seeds and membrane. Chop pepper; mix with garlic. Stir in remaining 1 teaspoon salt. Using mortar and pestle, grind mixture until smooth. Stir pepper mixture into eggplant mixture. Refrigerate, covered, 1 to 2 hours. Serve with pita bread.

12 servings.

CRAB DIP

LIZ OLIVER
CHARLOTTE, NORTH CAROLINA

⅓ cup unsweetened coconut milk

3 green onions, chopped

1 teaspoon minced jalapeño chiles

½ cup chopped fresh cilantro

½ cup mayonnaise

3 tablespoons fresh lime juice

1 lb. canned lump crabmeat, drained, flaked

❶ In blender, combine coconut milk, green onions, chile and ¼ cup of the cilantro; process until smooth. Stir in mayonnaise, lime juice, crabmeat and remaining ¼ cilantro. Serve dip with plantain chips, if desired.

12 servings.

SHRIMP DIP

NANCY HROMADA
AFTON, NEW YORK

2 (8-oz.) pkg. cream cheese, softened

½ cup chili sauce

2 tablespoons Worcestershire sauce

2 tablespoons French dressing

2 tablespoons mayonnaise or salad dressing

2 tablespoons prepared horseradish

1 onion, finely chopped

1 teaspoon garlic salt

Dash of hot pepper sauce

2 (8-oz.) cans cooked shrimp, drained

❶ In medium bowl, combine cream cheese, chili sauce, Worcestershire sauce, French dressing, mayonnaise, horseradish, onion, garlic and hot pepper sauce; mix well. Fold in shrimp; combine well. Refrigerate, covered, several hours before serving.

24 servings.

CRAB DIP

CREAM CHEESE SAUCE DIP

MICHELLE MORRILL
PRESCOTT VALLEY, ARIZONA

1 (8-oz.) jar apple jelly

1 (8-oz.) jar pineapple preserves

3 tablespoons dry mustard

3 tablespoons prepared horseradish

1 teaspoon freshly ground pepper

1 (8-oz.) pkg. cream cheese, softened.

❶ In large bowl, combine jelly, preserves, mustard, horseradish and pepper; mix well. Spread jelly mixture evenly over cream cheese. Serve with crackers.

12 servings.

SPINACH DIP

GERALD ROEDER
MOCKSVILLE, NORTH CAROLINA

1 (10-oz.) pkg. frozen chopped spinach, thawed, drained

1½ cups sour cream

1 cup mayonnaise

1 (14-oz.) pkg. dry vegetable soup mix

1 (8-oz.) can water chestnuts, drained, chopped

3 green onions, chopped

❶ In medium bowl combine spinach, sour cream, mayonnaise, soup mix, water chestnuts and green onions; mix well. Refrigerate, covered, until ready to serve. Serve with fresh vegetables, crackers or chips, if desired.

12 servings.

ARTICHOKE AND FETA DIP

CAROLYN LYONS
BROCKTON, MASSACHUSETTS

1 (6-oz.) can marinated artichoke hearts, drained, coarsely chopped

1 garlic clove, minced, plus 1 teaspoon minced

1 anchovy fillet, minced

½ cup sour cream

⅓ cup crumbled feta cheese

¼ teaspoon freshly ground pepper

½ teaspoon kosher (coarse) salt

1 teaspoon chopped fresh dill

Fresh dill sprigs

❶ In medium bowl, gently combine artichoke hearts, garlic, anchovy, sour cream, feta cheese, pepper, salt, and dill. Serve immediately or refrigerate, covered, up to 4 hours. Garnish with dill sprigs. Serve with pita triangles or fresh vegetables, if desired.

8 servings.

PRAIRIE FIRE BEAN DIP

SUSAN PAUL
PRINCETON, MINNESOTA

2 tablespoons unsalted butter

3 tablespoons corn oil

1/2 onion, finely chopped

2 garlic cloves, minced

2 (15-oz.) cans pinto beans, drained, 1/3 cup juice reserved

2 cups (8 oz.) grated Monterey Jack or cheddar cheese

1 (4-oz.) can chopped jalapeño chiles, undrained

Tortilla chips

❶ In large skillet, heat butter and oil over medium-high heat. Add onion and garlic; sauté 5 minutes or until onion is tender. Add beans; mash with potato masher. Stir in cheese and chiles. Continue to cook 5 minutes, stirring frequently, until cheese is melted. Serve in slow cooker, chafing dish or other heated serving dish with tortilla chips.

12 servings.

HOT CRAB DIP

JESSICA WEST BRATCHER
ROCKPORT, INDIANA

1 (8-oz.) pkg. cream cheese

1/4 cup mayonnaise or salad dressing

1/4 teaspoon garlic powder

1 teaspoon onion powder

1 teaspoon ground mustard

1 teaspoon sugar

1/2 lb. canned lump crabmeat, drained, flaked

1 large bread round (French, Italian, rye or wheat)

❶ Heat oven to 350°F.

❷ In oven-safe bowl, combine cream cheese, mayonnaise, garlic powder, onion powder, mustard, sugar and crabmeat; stir together until creamy. Bake mixture 20 to 25 minutes or until lightly browned on top and bubbly.

❸ Hollow out bread loaf, tearing soft bread into 1-inch pieces. Pour hot crab dip into bread bowl. Surround bread bowl with bread bits on platter. Serve dip hot.

10 servings.

Pastries, Quiches, Turnovers & Tarts

SWISS SPINACH QUICHE

JOYCE LEY
WEXFORD, PENNSYLVANIA

1 (8-oz.) can refrigerated crescent roll dough

1 (8-oz.) pkg. Swiss cheese slices, cut into thin strips

1/2 cup (2 oz.) freshly grated Parmesan cheese

3 tablespoons all-purpose flour

1 1/4 cups milk

4 eggs, slightly beaten

1/4 teaspoon salt

1/8 teaspoon freshly ground pepper

1/8 teaspoon nutmeg

1 (10-oz.) pkg. frozen chopped spinach, thawed, drained

❶ Heat oven to 350°F. Spray 13x9-inch pan with nonstick cooking spray.

❷ Separate crescent dough into rectangles. Place rectangles in bottom of pan. Press dough into bottom and 1/4 inch up sides of pan.

❸ In medium bowl, toss cheeses and flour. In another medium bowl, combine milk, eggs, salt, pepper and nutmeg; mix well. Add cheese mixture to milk mixture; mix well. Stir in spinach. Pour mixture into crust. Bake 40 to 50 minutes or until knife inserted near center comes out clean.

24 servings.

CREAMY CHICKEN FILLED EMPANADAS

RAQUEL PRYSZCZUK
PALO ALTO, CALIFORNIA

DOUGH

3 1/2 cups all-purpose flour

1 1/2 teaspoons salt

1 1/2 teaspoons paprika

1 1/2 cups butter

6 to 8 tablespoons water

FILLING

2 tablespoons butter

1 small onion, minced

2 boneless skinless chicken breast halves, minced

1 (8-oz.) pkg. cream cheese

1/8 teaspoon salt

1/8 teaspoon freshly ground pepper

❶ Heat oven to 350°F.

❷ In food processor, combine flour, salt and paprika. Cut in 1 1/2 cups butter until mixture crumbles. Stir in enough water to form soft dough. Shape dough into 5 equal balls.

❸ In large skillet, melt 2 tablespoons butter over medium heat. Add onion; sauté until tender. Stir in chicken, cream cheese, salt and pepper; cool.

❹ On lightly floured surface, roll out dough thinly, one ball at a time. With 2 1/2 -inch round cutter, cut dough into circles. Spoon heaping tablespoon filling into middle of each pastry circle, leaving 1/4-inch border. Fold one side of circle over filling so that edges meet, forming a half circle. Seal by pressing edges with fingertips, then pressing edges with tines of fork. Repeat until all empanadas are folded and sealed.

❺ Arrange empanadas on baking sheet. Bake 15 to 20 minutes or until golden brown.

20 servings.

MUSHROOM PALMIERS

KATHLEEN MAXWELL
SYLVANIA, OHIO

PALMIERS
5 tablespoons unsalted butter

18 oz. mushrooms, very finely chopped

1 large onion, finely chopped

3/4 teaspoon fresh lemon juice

2 tablespoons all-purpose flour

3 tablespoons fresh thyme, chopped

2 tablespoons Madeira wine

1/4 teaspoon salt

1/4 teaspoon freshly ground pepper

3 frozen puff pastry sheets, thawed

GLAZE
2 pasteurized eggs, beaten

4 teaspoons water

❶ In large skillet, melt butter over medium-high heat. Add mushrooms and onions; cook 8 minutes or until juices evaporate, stirring occasionally. Mix in lemon juice, flour and thyme; stir 2 minutes. Stir in Madeira. Season with salt and pepper; cool.

❷ Spread one-third of mushroom mixture evenly over 1 pastry sheet. Starting from short side, roll up jelly-roll style to center. Starting at second short side, roll up to meet in center. Press 2 sides together; transfer to baking sheet. Repeat with remaining pastry sheets. Refrigerate, covered, at least 1 hour or overnight.

❸ In medium bowl, combine eggs and water. Brush cooked pastries with glaze.

❹ Heat oven to 400°F.

❺ Using serrated knife, slice pastry into 1/4-inch-thick slices. Arrange, cut side down, 1 inch apart on baking sheets. Bake 20 minutes or until golden brown.

20 servings.

SHRIMP PUFFS

LANNY WHITE
LA PORTE, TEXAS

SHELLS
1/2 cup all-purpose flour

1/4 teaspoon salt

1/2 cup hot water

1/4 cup shortening

2 eggs

SAUCE
1/4 cup butter, softened

1 1/2 tablespoons grated onion

1 1/2 tablespoons fresh lemon juice

1 tablespoon prepared mustard

1 garlic clove, crushed

1 tablespoon prepared horseradish

SHRIMP
3 dozen shelled, deveined cooked small shrimp

❶ Heat oven to 350°F. Spray baking sheet with non-stick cooking spray.

❷ In medium bowl, sift together flour and salt. In medium saucepan, bring shortening and water to a boil over medium heat. Add flour mixture; stir until mixture leaves sides of pan. Remove from heat.

❸ Add eggs, one at a time, beating well with each addition. Drop mixture by rounded teaspoon onto baking sheet. Bake 10 minutes. Reduce heat to 350°F. Cook an additional 15 minutes or until golden.

❹ In small bowl, combine butter, onion, lemon juice, mustard, garlic and horseradish; mix well. After shells have cooled, cut tops off (shells will be hollow). Put 1/2 teaspoon of the butter mixture inside each shell. Add 1 shrimp on top of butter mixture, keeping shrimp upright in shell. Arrange shrimp puffs on baking sheet. Bake 1 to 2 minutes or until butter has melted.

12 servings.

PIZZA CUPS

ROSEMARY LEES
NORTH ROYALTON, OHIO

1/2 lb. bulk Italian sausage

1 cup pizza sauce

1 (7.5-oz.) can refrigerated biscuit dough

3/4 cup (3 oz.) shredded Mozzarella cheese

❶ In large skillet, cook sausage over medium heat until no longer pink; drain. Add pizza sauce; simmer, uncovered, stirring frequently, 15 minutes. Set aside.

❷ Heat oven to 400°F. Spray 10 cups of 12-cup muffin pan with nonstick cooking spray. Separate biscuit dough, placing 1 biscuit in each cup. Press dough into bottom and up sides of each cup. Let stand 2 minutes to shrink down. Press again.

❸ Spoon sausage mixture into each cup. Sprinkle with cheese. Bake 10 to 12 minutes or until golden.

5 servings.

SAUSAGE STARS

ALBERTA DEVRIES
PELLA, IOWA

1 lb. bulk pork sausage, cooked, crumbled, drained

1 1/2 cups (6 oz.) shredded sharp cheddar cheese

1 1/2 cups (6 oz.) shredded Monterey Jack cheese

1 (3.8-oz.) can sliced ripe olives, drained

1 cup ranch dressing

1/2 cup chopped red bell peppers

1 (1-lb.) pkg. wonton wrappers

❶ Heat oven to 350°F. Spray 12 (1¾-inch) miniature muffin cups with nonstick cooking spray. You will have to bake stars in batches.

❷ In large bowl, combine sausage, cheeses, olives, dressing and bell peppers; mix well.

❸ Press 1 wonton wrapper into each muffin cup. Brush with oil. Bake 5 minutes or until crisp and golden. Transfer wontons to baking sheet. Fill cups evenly with sausage mixture. Bake an additional 5 minutes.

6 servings.

BAKED ONION TURNOVERS

CHRIS McBEE
XENIA, OHIO

PASTRY

2 1/2 cups all-purpose flour

1 teaspoon dry mustard

1/2 teaspoon salt

1/8 teaspoon crushed red pepper

2 (8-oz.) pkg. cream cheese, softened

3/4 cup margarine, softened

FILLING

2 tablespoons butter

6 cups coarsely chopped yellow onions

2 tablespoons packed brown sugar

1/2 teaspoon salt

1/4 teaspoon freshly ground pepper

1/4 teaspoon curry powder

1/8 teaspoon crushed red pepper

❶ In medium bowl, combine flour, mustard, salt and red pepper; mix well. In food processor, blend cream cheese and margarine. Add flour mixture to cream cheese mixture; blend.

❷ Divide dough into fourths. Wrap in plastic wrap; refrigerate dough 1 hour.

❸ Heat oven to 375°F.

❹ In large skillet, melt butter over medium-high heat. Add onions; sauté until tender. Stir in brown sugar. Cook an additional 5 minutes or until onions are light brown and sugar is dissolved. Remove from heat; stir in salt, black pepper, curry powder and red pepper.

❺ On floured surface, roll out one-fourth of the dough into 9-inch square. Cut into 3-inch squares. Place about 1 rounded teaspoon of onion mixture in center of each square. Fold dough over filling to form a triangle, using fork to crimp edges together. Turn pastries over and crimp edges again. Arrange pastries on greased baking sheet. Bake 15 to 20 minutes or until lightly browned. Serve warm.

12 servings.

MUSHROOM CROUSTADES

FRAN BERTAPELLE
McLEAN, VIRGINIA

CROUSTADES
2 tablespoons butter, softened
24 thin slices fresh white bread

FILLING
4 tablespoons butter
3 tablespoons finely chopped shallots
1/2 lb. fresh mushrooms, finely chopped
3 tablespoons all-purpose flour
1 cup whipping cream
1/2 teaspoon salt
1/8 teaspoon cayenne pepper
1/4 cup chopped fresh parsley
1/3 cup chives
1/2 teaspoon fresh lemon juice
2 tablespoons freshly grated Parmesan cheese
1 tablespoon butter, cut into small pieces

❶ Heat oven to 375°F. Coat inside of 24 (2-inch) muffin cups with 2 tablespoons butter.

❷ Using 3-inch round cutter, cut out circle from each bread slice. Press each circle gently, but firmly, into bottom and up sides of muffin cup. Bake 10 minutes or until bread is golden brown.

❸ In medium skillet, melt 4 tablespoons butter over medium heat. Add shallots; cook 10 minutes, stirring frequently. Add mushrooms; increase heat to medium-high. Cook 8 to 10 minutes, stirring frequently, until liquid of mushrooms is evaporated. Remove skillet from heat. Sprinkle flour over mushrooms and stir. Return skillet to medium heat. Gradually stir in cream. Simmer, stirring constantly, 2 to 3 minutes or until mixture thickens. Remove from heat; stir in salt, cayenne, parsley, chives and lemon juice.

❹ Reduce oven temperature to 350°F. Place croustades on baking sheet. Fill each croustade with heaping teaspoon of the mushroom filling. Sprinkle with Parmesan cheese; dot with 1 tablespoon butter. Bake 10 minutes or until heated through.

12 servings.

SALMON TARTS

MICHELLE MORRILL
PRESCOTT VALLEY, ARIZONA

1 1/2 cups baking mix
1/2 cup milk
1/4 cup sour cream
1/2 teaspoon Worcestershire sauce
2 eggs
2/3 cup shredded cheddar cheese
1/2 cup canned salmon, drained, flaked
2 green onions, chopped

❶ Heat oven to 400°F. Lightly spray 24 (1¾-inch) miniature muffin cups with nonstick cooking spray.

❷ In large bowl, beat baking mix, milk, sour cream, Worcestershire sauce and eggs at medium speed until well blended. Fold in cheese, salmon and green onions.

❸ Spoon 1 tablespoon mixture into bottom and up sides of each muffin cup.

❹ Bake 20 minutes or until golden. Cool 5 minutes; remove from pan. Serve warm.

12 servings.

ASIAN PHYLLO PURSES

ASIAN PHYLLO PURSES

CAROLYN LINSLEY
PITTSBURGH, PENNSYLVANIA

2 tablespoons oil

3/4 lb. boneless skinless chicken breast halves, diced (1/4 inch)

1/2 cup sliced green onions

1 (5-oz.) can sliced water chestnuts, drained, diced (1/4 inch)

1/2 cup bottled stir-fry sauce

10 sheets frozen phyllo pastry, thawed

❶ Heat oven to 350°F.

❷ In large skillet, heat oil over medium-high heat until hot. Add chicken; stir-fry 1 minute or until no longer pink. Add green onions and water chestnuts; stir-fry an additional minute or until chicken is no longer pink in center. Stir in sauce; stir-fry until liquid has evaporated to a glaze. Set aside.

❸ Peel 2 sheets phyllo from stack, keeping remaining sheets covered with parchment paper and damp towel. Place the 2 sheets, one on top of the other, on a greased surface. Spray top phyllo sheet with cooking spray.

❹ Cut 2 sheets in half horizontally, then in half vertically. Cut each rectangle into 3 rectangles.

❺ Place 1 teaspoon of the filling in center of each dough rectangle. Gather dough around filling; twist like a drawstring purse, working gently to avoid tearing. Place bundles on 15x10x1-inch baking pan. Bake 12 to 15 minutes or until brown.

16 servings.

PEPPERONI CHEESE MINI-MUFFINS

DAVID AND PATRICIA RITTER
DOUGLASSVILLE, PENNSYLVANIA

2 cups all-purpose flour

2 eggs

1 1/2 cups milk

1 tightly packed cup diced pepperoni

1 1/2 cups (6 oz.) shredded sharp cheddar cheese

1/3 cup grated mozzarella or Parmesan cheese

1 teaspoon baking powder

❶ Heat oven to 400°F. Spray 12 (1 3/4-inch) miniature muffin cups with nonstick cooking spray.

❷ In large bowl, combine flour, eggs, milk, pepperoni, cheeses and baking powder; mix well. Drop mixture by teaspoonfuls into muffin cups.

❸ Bake 15 to 20 minutes or until golden brown. Serve hot.

6 servings.

HOT CHEESE PUFFS

FLORENCE BOGSTAD
NORTHRIDGE, CALIFORNIA

1 cup water

1/4 cup butter

1 cup all-purpose flour

1/2 teaspoon salt

4 eggs

3/4 cup (3 oz.) shredded cheddar cheese

3/4 cup (3 oz.) freshly grated Parmesan cheese

❶ Heat oven to 350°F. Spray baking sheet with nonstick cooking spray.

❷ In medium saucepan, boil water and butter over medium-high heat until butter is melted. Remove saucepan from heat; add flour and salt, stirring vigorously with wooden spoon until mixture leaves sides of pan. Add eggs, one at a time, beating well with each addition. Add cheeses; mix thoroughly.

❸ Drop dough by teaspoonfuls onto baking sheet. Bake 15 minutes or until lightly browned.

12 servings.

HAM AND ARTICHOKE CROUSTADES

BARBARA ASCHENBRENNER
LOS ALTOS, CALIFORNIA

CROUSTADES

12 to 18 slices homemade-style white bread
4 tablespoons unsalted butter, melted

FILLING

3 tablespoons unsalted butter
1/2 cup finely chopped onions
2 tablespoons all-purpose flour
1 cup milk
1/2 cup (2 oz.) grated sharp cheddar cheese
1/2 cup finely diced ham
1/2 cup marinated artichoke hearts, drained, diced
2 teaspoons Dijon-style mustard
1/2 teaspoon dried sage
1/8 teaspoon salt
1/8 teaspoon freshly ground pepper

❶ Heat oven to 375°F.

❷ Flatten each bread slice with rolling pin. With 2¼-inch round cutter, cut out 2 or 3 circles from each slice. Press each bread circle into bottom of 36 (1¾-inch) buttered miniature muffin cups. Brush with melted butter.

❸ Bake 6 minutes or until pale golden. Cool in muffin cups on wire racks 5 minutes. Remove from pans; cool completely on racks.

❹ In large skillet, melt 1 tablespoon butter over medium heat. Add onions; sauté 5 minutes or until tender. Set aside. In medium saucepan, melt 2 tablespoons butter over medium heat. Add flour; cook, whisking constantly, 2 minutes. Add milk in a steady stream, whisking constantly; bring mixture to a boil. Simmer mixture over medium-low heat. Add cheese, ham, artichokes, sautéed onions, mustard, sage, salt and pepper. Stir mixture until well combined.

❺ Spoon 1 to 2 teaspoons of the mixture into each bread "shell," smoothing the top into a mound. Arrange filled shells on baking sheet. Bake 10 to 15 minutes or until tops are golden.

18 servings.

SAVORY CHEESECAKES

KATRINA NIGRO
HOLLAND, NEW YORK

1/4 cup fine dry bread crumbs
1/4 cup ground pecans, toasted
2 tablespoons butter, melted
1 (8-oz.) pkg. cream cheese, softened
1 egg
2 tablespoons milk
2 tablespoons hot pepper sauce
1/4 cup green bell pepper jelly, melted
1/4 cup hot red jalapeño chile jelly, melted

❶ In large bowl, combine bread crumbs, pecans and butter; mix well. Line 24 (1¾-inch) miniature muffin cups with paper baking cups. Spoon and press about 1 teaspoon crumb mixture evenly into bottom of each cup.

❷ In medium bowl, beat cream cheese at medium speed until light and fluffy. Add egg and milk, beating until just blended. Stir in hot pepper sauce. Spoon mixture into paper cups, filling three-fourths full. Bake 10 minutes or until set. Let cheesecakes cool completely in pans; cover and refrigerate.

❸ Spoon ½ teaspoon melted bell pepper jelly over 12 cheesecakes. Spoon ½ teaspoon chile jelly evenly over remaining 12 cheesecakes. Refrigerate, covered, until chilled.

12 servings.

SAUSAGE ROLLS

CHRIS McBEE
XENIA, OHIO

PASTRY
2 cups all-purpose flour
¼ teaspoon salt
¾ cup butter, chilled, cut into ½-inch squares
4 to 6 tablespoons ice water

FILLING
2 lb. bulk pork sausage
1 tablespoon finely chopped fresh sage
1½ tablespoons finely chopped fresh thyme or 1½ teaspoons dried
1 teaspoon freshly ground pepper
½ teaspoon ground allspice
1 egg, beaten

❶ Sift flour with ¼ teaspoon salt into food processor. Add butter and water; pulse quickly until roughly mixed. Turn onto lightly floured board; with hands, shape mixture into ball. Roll out 8x10-inch rectangle; fold into thirds, as if an envelope, and give it a half turn to bring the open edge to the front. Repeat rolling and turning process twice more, giving the pastry three turns in all. Wrap in plastic wrap; refrigerate 1 hour.

❷ Heat oven to 425°F.

❸ In large bowl, combine sausage, sage, thyme, pepper and allspice.

❹ Cut pastry in half; roll into 8x12-inch rectangle, about ⅛ inch thick. Cut pastry in half lengthwise. Roll sausage mixture into 1-inch diameter cylinders to cover the length of the pastry. With pastry brush, lightly coat surface of each strip of pastry with water. Place sausage near long edge and roll up, finishing with the cut edge underneath. Brush roll with egg; cut into 1-inch pieces. With sharp knife, make 2 small slashes on top of each sausage roll. Place rolls on baking sheet.

❺ Bake 25 to 30 minutes or until sausage is no longer pink in center and pastry is golden brown. Serve hot or at room temperature with a honey-mustard sauce, if desired.

24 servings.

CHICKEN NUT PUFFS

PEGGY YAMAGUCHI-LAZAR
EUGENE, OREGON

1½ cups diced cooked chicken
⅓ cup chopped almonds, toasted
1 cup canned reduced-sodium chicken broth
½ cup vegetable oil
2 teaspoons Worcestershire sauce
1 tablespoon dried parsley
1 teaspoon seasoned salt
½ teaspoon celery seed
⅛ teaspoon cayenne pepper
1 cup all-purpose flour
4 large eggs

❶ Heat oven to 450°F. Spray baking sheet with non-stick cooking spray.

❷ In medium bowl, combine chicken and almonds. Set aside.

❸ In large saucepan, combine broth, oil, Worcestershire sauce, parsley, salt, celery seed and cayenne; bring to a boil over medium-high heat. Add flour, stirring until smooth ball forms. Remove saucepan from heat; let stand 5 minutes. Add eggs, one at a time, beating well after each addition until dough is smooth. Stir in chicken and almonds.

❹ Drop chicken mixture by heaping teaspoonfuls onto baking sheet. Bake 12 to 14 minutes or until golden brown. Serve warm.

24 servings.

SPINACH QUICHELETS

CHARLOTTE WARD
HILTON HEAD ISLAND, SOUTH CAROLINA

DOUGH

½ lb. margarine

6 oz. cream cheese, softened

2 cups all-purpose flour

FILLING

1 (10-oz.) pkg. frozen chopped spinach, thawed, drained

1½ cups (6 oz.) shredded Swiss cheese

4 eggs

1½ tablespoons all-purpose flour

2 (.06-oz.) envelopes dry cream of chicken soup mix

1 (5-oz.) can evaporated milk

¼ teaspoon nutmeg

⅛ teaspoon freshly ground pepper

Pimientos

❶ Spray 48 (1¾-inch) miniature muffin cups with nonstick cooking spray.

❷ In medium bowl, beat margarine and cream cheese until combined. Gradually add flour. Form mixture into 48 balls; refrigerate 12 hours.

❸ Heat oven to 375°F. Place 1 ball in each muffin cup. Press center with thumb. Divide spinach and cheese evenly among muffin cups.

❹ In blender, combine eggs, flour, soup mix, milk, nutmeg and pepper; process until smooth. Pour mixture over spinach and cheese, filling three-fourths full.

❺ Bake 18 to 20 minutes or until set. Garnish with pimientos. Serve immediately or at room temperature.

24 servings.

TRIOPETAS

ROBERT EAMES
TAUNTON, MASSACHUSETTS

½ lb. crumbled Danish blue cheese

1 (3-oz.) pkg. cream cheese, softened

¼ cup (1 oz.) freshly grated Romano cheese

2 hard-cooked eggs, finely chopped

1 (2-oz.) can anchovy fillets, drained, chopped

3 to 4 dashes hot pepper sauce

⅛ teaspoon nutmeg

1 (16-oz.) pkg. frozen phyllo pastry, thawed

1 cup butter, melted

❶ Heat oven to 350°F.

❷ In large bowl, combine blue cheese, cream cheese, Romano cheese, eggs, anchovy fillets, hot pepper sauce and nutmeg; mix well.

❸ Layer 2 phyllo sheets together, brushing each with butter. Cut lengthwise strips about 2½ inches wide. Place 1 teaspoon filling on bottom corner; fold in triangle shape and continue folding the whole strip as you would fold a flag. Brush tops with butter. Repeat with remaining phyllo and filling. Bake 15 to 20 minutes or until golden brown.

24 servings.

SHRIMP PUFFS

RENAY WULPERN
SANFORD, NORTH CAROLINA

DOUGH
1 cup water
½ cup butter
1 cup all-purpose flour
4 eggs

FILLING
¼ lb. shelled, deveined cooked medium shrimp, chopped
1 cup (4 oz.) shredded sharp cheddar cheese
⅓ cup grated onions
1 cup mayonnaise
1 teaspoon Worcestershire sauce

❶ Heat oven to 375°F. Spray baking sheet with non-stick cooking spray.

❷ In medium saucepan, heat water and butter over medium-high heat until mixture boils. Remove saucepan from heat. Add flour. With wooden spoon, stir until mixture leaves side of pan and forms a ball. Add eggs, one at a time, beating well until dough is smooth.

❸ Spoon dough into pastry bag fitted with large round tip. Pipe balls onto baking sheet about 2 inches apart. Bake 20 minutes or until golden. Remove to wire rack to cool. While puffs are cooling, prepare filling.

❹ In large bowl, combine shrimp, cheese, onions, mayonnaise and Worcestershire sauce; mix well. Refrigerate, covered, 30 minutes. Slice top off each puff; fill with 1 teaspoon of filling. Replace top and arrange on serving plate.

12 servings.

BRIE AND MUSHROOM TARTLETS

BARBARA ASCHENBRENNER
LOS ALTOS, CALIFORNIA

Butter-flavored nonstick cooking spray
30 to 36 round wonton skins
1 tablespoon olive oil
2 tablespoons unsalted butter
½ cup minced onions
2 garlic cloves, minced
½ lb. mushrooms, finely chopped
1 tablespoon dry sherry
1 teaspoon balsamic vinegar
1 teaspoon Worcestershire sauce
1 teaspoon fresh lemon juice
Dash of cayenne pepper
⅛ teaspoon salt
⅛ teaspoon freshly ground pepper
8 oz. Brie cheese

❶ Heat oven to 350°F. Spray 36 (1¾-inch) miniature muffin cups with cooking spray.

❷ Press 1 wonton skin into each cup; lightly brush with olive oil. Bake 7 to 10 minutes or until light brown. Remove from muffin cups; set aside to cool.

❸ In large skillet, melt butter over medium heat. Add onions; sauté 4 to 6 minutes or until tender. Add garlic; sauté 1 to 2 minutes or until fragrant. Add mushrooms, sherry, balsamic vinegar, Worcestershire sauce, lemon juice, cayenne, salt and pepper; sauté 2 to 4 minutes or until liquid of mushrooms is evaporated. Cool mushroom mixture.

❹ Press generous teaspoon of cheese into each wonton; top with a generous teaspoonful of mushroom mixture. Arrange wontons on baking sheet. Bake 10 minutes or until warmed though and cheese is bubbly. Serve immediately.

18 servings.

PEPPERONI CHEESE BITES

DAVID AND PATRICIA RITTER
DOUGLASSVILLE, PENNSYLVANIA

¼ lb. very thin slices pepperoni
1 (10-oz.) pkg. frozen chopped spinach, thawed, drained
1 (15-oz.) container ricotta cheese
1½ cups (6 oz.) freshly grated Parmesan cheese
1½ cups fresh mushrooms, finely chopped
¼ cup finely chopped onions
1 teaspoon dried oregano
2 eggs, lightly beaten

❶ Heat oven to 375°F. In each of 36 (1¾-inch) miniature muffin cups, rub 1 pepperoni slice around cup to lightly grease; press slice into bottom of muffin cup. (*Any remaining pepperoni slices can be cut into wedges for topping.*)

❷ In large bowl, combine spinach, ricotta, Parmesan, mushrooms, onion, oregano and eggs; mix until blended and stiff. Spoon and press mixture into muffin cups, mounding slightly above top of pan. (*The mixture does not rise during baking.*)

❸ Bake 20 to 25 minutes or until lightly browned. Remove pans from oven; cool at least 10 minutes before carefully removing from pans. Serve warm.

18 servings.

CHICKARITOS

CHRIS McBEE
XENIA, OHIO

3 cups diced cooked chicken
1½ cups (6 oz.) shredded sharp cheddar cheese
1 (4-oz.) can chopped green chiles
½ cup finely chopped green onions
1 teaspoon hot pepper sauce
1 teaspoon garlic salt
¼ teaspoon freshly ground pepper
¼ teaspoon ground cumin
¼ teaspoon paprika
1 (17.25-oz.) pkg. frozen puff pastry sheets, thawed

❶ Heat oven to 425°F. Spray baking sheet with non-stick cooking spray.

❷ In large bowl, combine chicken, cheese, chiles, onions and seasonings; mix well. Refrigerate mixture until ready to use.

❸ Remove half of the pastry from refrigerator at a time, keeping remaining pastry covered. On lightly floured surface, roll pastry into 12x9-inch rectangle. Cut into 9 small rectangles. Place about 2 tablespoonfuls filling down center of each rectangle. Wet edges of pastry with water; roll pastry around filling. Crimp ends with fork to seal. Repeat with remaining pastry and filling. Place seam side down on baking sheet. Refrigerate until ready to bake.

❹ Bake 20 to 25 minutes or until golden brown. Serve warm with guacamole and salsa.

18 servings.

GROUND BEEF SNACK QUICHES

**PEGGY YAMAGUCHI-LAZAR
EUGENE, OREGON**

¼ lb. ground beef

¼ teaspoon garlic powder

¼ teaspoon freshly ground pepper

1 cup baking mix

¼ cup cornmeal

¼ cup butter, chilled

2 to 3 tablespoons boiling water

1 large egg

½ cup half-and-half

1 tablespoon chopped green onions

1 tablespoon chopped red bell pepper

⅛ to ¼ teaspoon salt

¼ teaspoon cayenne pepper

½ cup (2 oz.) finely shredded cheddar cheese

❶ Heat oven to 375°F. Spray 16 (1¾-inch) miniature muffin cups with nonstick cooking spray.

❷ In medium saucepan, cook beef, garlic powder and black pepper over medium heat until meat is no longer pink in center. Drain and set aside.

❸ In medium bowl, combine baking mix and cornmeal. Cut in butter. Add enough boiling water to form soft dough. Press dough evenly into bottom and up sides of muffin cups. Place teaspoonfuls of beef mixture into each shell.

❹ In another medium bowl, combine egg, half-and-half, green onion, bell pepper, salt and cayenne; mix well. Pour egg mixture over beef; sprinkle with cheese. Bake 20 minutes or until knife inserted near center comes out clean.

8 servings.

CHICKEN PUFFS

**BRANDIE DETMERING
BELLEVUE, NEBRASKA**

PASTRY

⅔ cup water

⅓ cup butter

⅔ cup all-purpose flour

⅛ teaspoon salt

3 eggs

3 tablespoons freshly grated Parmesan cheese

FILLING

½ cup finely chopped celery

2 tablespoons sweet pickle relish

⅛ teaspoon freshly ground pepper

½ cup seedless grapes, sliced

¼ cup mayonnaise

¼ teaspoon salt

2 tablespoons chopped almonds

1½ cups diced cooked chicken

❶ Heat oven to 400°F. Spray baking sheet with nonstick cooking spray. In medium saucepan, combine water and butter; bring to a boil over medium-high heat. Add flour and salt, stirring vigorously until mixture leaves sides of saucepan and forms a smooth ball. Remove from heat; cool 1 minute.

❷ Add eggs, one at a time, beating well after each addition. Beat until dough is smooth. Stir in Parmesan cheese.

❸ Spoon dough into pastry bag fitted with #5 or 6B fluted tip. Pipe dough into 30 small balls onto baking sheet. Bake 20 minutes or until puffed and golden brown; cool.

❹ Meanwhile, in large bowl, combine celery, pickle relish, pepper, grapes, mayonnaise, salt, almonds and chicken; mix well. Cut off top one-third of each puff. Remove and discard soft dough inside. Spoon filling into puffs. Replace tops. Insert decorative toothpick through center to secure. Refrigerate 1 hour before serving.

10 servings.

SPICY CHEESE SQUARES

RUTH COWLEY
BOERNE, TEXAS

2 cups (8 oz.) grated Monterey Jack cheese

2 cups (8 oz.) grated cheddar cheese

1 (4-oz.) can chopped green chiles, drained

Chopped pickled jalapeño chiles, if desired

2 cups milk

1 cup baking mix

4 eggs, beaten

1/2 cup salsa

❶ Heat oven to 425°F. Spray 13x9-inch pan with nonstick cooking spray.

❷ Sprinkle cheeses into bottom of pan. Top with chiles. In medium bowl, beat milk, baking mix and eggs at medium speed until smooth. Pour milk mixture over chiles. Top with salsa.

❸ Bake 25 to 30 minutes or until puffed and golden. Cut into 11/2x11/2-inch squares.

48 servings.

MINI SHRIMP QUICHES

CHARLOTTE WARD
HILTON HEAD ISLAND, SOUTH CAROLINA

DOUGH

1/2 lb. margarine

6 oz. cream cheese, softened

2 cups all-purpose flour

FILLING

11/2 cups shelled, deveined cooked small shrimp

11/2 cups (6 oz.) grated Swiss cheese

2 eggs

1 cup whipping cream

1 teaspoon dill seed or 1 tablespoon chopped fresh dill

1/2 cup (2 oz.) freshly grated Parmesan cheese

❶ In large bowl, beat margarine and cream cheese at medium speed until well blended. Gradually add flour. With hands, shape mixture into 48 balls; refrigerate, covered, 12 hours.

❷ Heat oven to 425°F. Press each pastry ball into bottom and up sides of 24 (13/4-inch) miniature muffin cups. Divide shrimp evenly among muffin cups. Sprinkle Swiss cheese evenly over shrimp.

❸ In medium bowl, beat eggs at medium speed until frothy. Stir in cream and dill. Spoon egg mixture evenly over shrimp and cheese. Sprinkle with Parmesan cheese.

❹ Bake 5 minutes. Reduce oven temperature to 350°F. Bake an additional 15 minutes or until golden brown. Served immediately or at room temperature.

12 servings.

MUSHROOM-BROCCOLI QUICHE BITES

BARBARA BRANDEL
LAKELAND, FLORIDA

1 loaf fresh white bread, sliced

2 eggs

1/4 cup milk

1/4 teaspoon baking powder

1 teaspoon dried parsley

1/8 teaspoon dried thyme

1/4 teaspoon salt

Dash of freshly ground pepper

1/3 cup finely chopped broccoli

1/3 cup shredded cheddar cheese

1/4 cup finely chopped fresh mushrooms

1 tablespoon finely chopped onion

❶ Heat broiler. Spray 24 (1¾-inch) miniature muffin cups with nonstick cooking spray.

❷ Roll bread slices with rolling pin between layers of damp paper toweling. Using 3-inch round cutter, cut circles from bread; press into bottom of muffin cups. *(If bread tears, use bread scraps to fill in.)*

❸ Broil 6 inches from heat 3 to 5 minutes or until edges begin to turn brown. Remove from broiler; cool.

❹ Heat oven to 350°F.

❺ In large bowl, combine eggs, milk, baking powder, parsley, thyme, salt and pepper; mix until well blended. Add broccoli, cheese, mushrooms and onion; mix well. Fill each crust with 1 teaspoon egg mixture. Bake 15 to 20 minutes or until filling is set.

12 servings.

HOT MUSHROOM TURNOVERS

LORI ELDRIDGE
LIMA, OHIO

3 (3-oz.) pkg. cream cheese, softened

1 1/2 cups plus 2 tablespoons all-purpose flour

1/2 cup plus 3 tablespoons butter, softened

1/2 lb. mushrooms, minced

1 medium onion, minced

2 garlic cloves, minced, if desired

1 teaspoon salt

1/4 teaspoon chopped fresh thyme

1/4 cup sour cream

1 egg, beaten

❶ In medium bowl, combine cream cheese, 1½ cups of the flour and ½ cup of the butter; mix well, scraping bowl occasionally. Wrap dough in plastic wrap; refrigerate 1 hour.

❷ In medium skillet, melt remaining 3 tablespoons butter over medium heat. Add mushrooms, onion and garlic; sauté until onion is tender. Stir in salt, thyme and remaining 2 tablespoons of the flour; mix well. Stir in sour cream.

❸ On floured surface, thinly roll out half of the dough at a time. With 2¾-inch round cutter, cut approximately 30 circles. Re roll scraps.

❹ On half of each circle, spread 1 teaspoonful of mushroom mixture. Brush edges with egg. Fold dough over filling. With fork, press edges together and prick tops. Arrange turnovers on ungreased baking sheets. Repeat with remaining dough and filling.

❺ Heat oven to 450°F. Brush turnovers with egg. Refrigerate 1 hour or until firm. Bake 12 minutes or until golden. Bake 12 minutes or until golden.

10 servings.

LITTLE FETA CHEESECAKES

CHARLOTTE WARD
HILTON HEAD ISLAND, SOUTH CAROLINA

CRUST
½ cup fine dry bread crumbs
½ cup ground pecans
¼ cup butter, softened

FILLING
1 (8-oz.) pkg. cream cheese, softened
4 oz. crumbled feta cheese
1 egg
2 tablespoons milk
⅛ teaspoon hot pepper sauce

TOPPING
½ cup tomato sauce
2 tablespoons tomato paste
1 tablespoon minced onion
1 small garlic clove, minced
¼ teaspoon dried basil
¼ teaspoon dried oregano
⅛ teaspoon freshly ground pepper
⅛ teaspoon crushed red pepper
⅛ teaspoon sugar
⅛ teaspoon grated lemon peel

❶ Heat oven to 350°F.

❷ In medium bowl, combine bread crumbs, pecans and butter; set aside. Line 48 (1¾-inch) miniature muffin cups with paper liners. Press about 1 teaspoon of the bread crumb mixture into bottom of each liner.

❸ In another medium bowl, beat cream cheese at medium speed until light and fluffy. Add feta cheese and egg; beat well. Add milk and hot pepper sauce, beating until just mixed. Spoon mixture evenly over bread mixture in paper liners. Bake 10 to 12 minutes or until egg is set and cakes are lightly browned. Cool. Cover and refrigerate.

❹ Meanwhile, in medium saucepan, cook tomato sauce, tomato paste, onion, garlic, basil, oregano, black pepper, red pepper, sugar and lemon peel over medium heat until thickened.

❺ Remove paper liners from cheesecakes. Arrange cheesecakes on large baking sheet. Spoon ¼ teaspoon of the tomato mixture on center of each cheesecake. Refrigerate, covered, until ready to serve.

24 servings.

CURRIED CHICKEN MORSELS

LISA KRAMER
DENTON, MARYLAND

FILLING
1 cup diced cooked chicken
¼ cup sliced almonds
¼ cup chopped red bell pepper
2 tablespoons sliced green onions
2 tablespoons chutney
½ teaspoon curry powder
⅓ cup mayonnaise

CRUST
2 (8-oz.) cans refrigerated crescent roll dough

❶ Heat oven to 350°F.

❷ In large bowl, combine chicken, almonds, bell pepper, green onions, chutney, curry powder and mayonnaise; mix well.

❸ Unroll crescent dough. Pinch perforations together, forming each roll into rectangle. Cut each rectangle into 8 squares. Place 1 tablespoon chicken mixture in center on each square. Fold into a triangle; press to seal.

❹ Bake on ungreased baking sheet 10 minutes or until golden brown.

8 servings.

PEPPER JELLY TURNOVERS

DIANA PROLLCOK
DEL CITY, OKLAHOMA

1 cup (4 oz.) shredded sharp cheddar cheese
1 cup all-purpose flour
¼ cup chilled butter, cut up
1 tablespoon ice water
⅓ cup pepper jelly or jalapeño jelly
⅓ cup diced ham

❶ Heat oven to 375°F.

❷ In food processor, combine cheese and flour. Add butter; process until mixture crumbles. Add water; mix just until dough holds together.

❸ Divide dough in half. Roll each half ⅛ inch thick between 2 sheets parchment paper. Using 2-inch round cutter, cut into circles.

❹ Transfer circles to baking sheet. Place ¼ teaspoon each of jelly and ham in center of each circle. Fold over; crimp edges with fork. Repeat with remaining dough, rerolling scraps. Bake 10 to 15 minutes or until golden. Transfer to wire rack to cool.

8 servings.

SPINACH TRIANGLES

KATRINA NIGRO
HOLLAND, NEW YORK

2 tablespoons butter
⅓ cup minced onion
1 (10-oz.) pkg. frozen chopped spinach, thawed
1 cup (4 oz.) freshly grated Parmesan cheese
¾ cup (3 oz.) shredded sharp cheddar cheese
1 egg, beaten
3 tablespoons fresh bread crumbs
½ teaspoon garlic powder
½ teaspoon cayenne pepper
¼ teaspoon salt
Dash of hot pepper sauce
½ (16-oz.) pkg. frozen phyllo pastry, thawed
1 cup butter, melted
Paprika
Fresh spinach leaves

❶ Heat oven to 325°F.

❷ In large skillet, melt 2 tablespoons butter over medium heat. Add onion; sauté until tender. Stir in spinach, Parmesan cheese, cheddar cheese, egg, bread crumbs, garlic powder, cayenne, salt and hot pepper sauce.

❸ Cut sheets of phyllo lengthwise into 3-inch strips. Working with 1 strip at a time, brush lightly with melted butter. (*Keep remaining phyllo covered with plastic wrap and damp kitchen towel*). Place 2 teaspoons spinach mixture at base of phyllo strip. Fold right bottom corner over to form a triangle. Continue folding back and forth into a triangle to end of strip. Repeat with remaining phyllo strips and spinach mixture.

❹ Arrange triangles, seam side down, on baking sheets. Brush tops with remaining melted butter. Bake 30 to 35 minutes or until triangles are lightly browned and flaky. Drain on paper towels. Sprinkle with paprika. Garnish with fresh spinach leaves.

20 servings.

OVEN-BAKED APPLE POCKETS

VIANEY HERNANDEZ
VAN NUYS, CALIFORNIA

CRUST
1 (17.25-oz.) pkg. frozen puff pastry dough, thawed

FILLING
1/2 cup golden raisins
1 tablespoon dark rum
1 lb. Granny Smith apples, cored, chopped
1 tablespoon fresh lemon juice
1/4 cup granulated sugar
1/2 teaspoon cinnamon
1/3 cup ground almonds
1 egg white

ICING
1/2 cup powdered sugar
1 tablespoon fresh lemon juice

❶ Separate pastry dough; roll each sheet out to 10x15 inches. Cut sheets into 6 (5-inch) squares.

❷ In medium bowl, combine raisins and rum; soak 30 minutes. Drain raisins, reserving rum.

❸ Heat oven to 400°F. In medium saucepan, simmer apples, 1 tablespoon lemon juice, granulated sugar, reserved rum and cinnamon 3 to 4 minutes or until apples soften; cool.

❹ Drop spoonfuls of apple mixture on half of each pastry square; sprinkle with almonds and rum-soaked raisins.

❺ In small bowl, beat egg white lightly. Using a pastry brush, gently coat edges without disturbing filling. Fold dough over filling; press edges firmly with fork to seal decoratively. Arrange pockets on baking sheet. Bake 25 minutes or until golden; cool.

❻ In another small bowl, whisk 1/2 cup powdered sugar and 1 tablespoon lemon juice until smooth. Brush glaze over pockets.

10 servings.

ARTICHOKE-PARMESAN PUFFS

CHRIS McBEE
XENIA, OHIO

1 cup water
2 tablespoons margarine
1 cup all-purpose flour
1 teaspoon garlic salt
1/2 cup fat-free cholesterol-free egg product
1 egg
1 (14-oz.) can artichoke hearts, drained, finely chopped
1/4 cup (1 oz.) freshly grated reduced-fat Parmesan cheese

❶ Heat oven to 375°F.

❷ Line baking sheet with parchment paper

❸ In large saucepan, bring water and margarine to a boil over medium-high heat. Reduce heat to low. Add flour and garlic salt, stirring vigorously, until mixture forms a ball; remove from heat. Add egg product and egg; beat until well blended. Beat in artichoke hearts and cheese.

❹ Drop mixture by heaping teaspoonfuls onto baking sheet. Bake 25 to 28 minutes or until lightly browned. Serve warm.

20 servings.

FRESH BARBECUE CUPS

MARILYN HICKS
CLEAR LAKE OAKS, CALIFORNIA

1 (10-oz.) can refrigerated biscuit dough

1 lb. ground beef

½ cup barbecue sauce

¼ cup chopped onions

1 to 2 tablespoons packed brown sugar

½ cup (2 oz.) shredded cheddar or American cheese

❶ Heat oven to 400°F. Spray 10 (2-inch) muffin cups with nonstick cooking spray.

❷ Place 1 biscuit in each cup, pressing firmly in bottom and up sides of cups. Form ¼-inch rim at top.

❸ In large skillet, cook beef over medium heat until no longer pink in center; drain. Stir in barbecue sauce, onions and sugar; cook, stirring constantly, one minute. Spoon ¼ cup meat mixture evenly into each muffin cup. Sprinkle each with cheese.

❹ Bake 10 to 15 minutes or until edges are golden. Cool 1 minute.

5 servings.

MINI QUICHE

ROBIN RICHEY
STERLING HEIGHTS, MICHIGAN

1 lb. spinach dip

½ lb. crumbled feta cheese

½ (17.25-oz.) pkg. frozen phyllo dough, thawed

½ cup melted butter

❶ Heat oven to 350°F.

❷ In medium bowl, combine spinach dip and feta cheese; mix well.

❸ Cut sheets of phyllo lengthwise into 3-inch strips. Working with 1 strip at a time, brush with melted butter. Place 2 teaspoons spinach mixture at base of phyllo strip. Fold right bottom corner over to form a triangle. Continue folding back and forth into a triangle to end of strip. Repeat with remaining phyllo strips and spinach mixture. Brush with butter.

❹ Arrange strips on baking sheet. Bake 15 to 20 minutes until golden.

10 servings.

Pizzas, Breads, Crackers & Crunchers

TAPENADE WITH PITA CRISPS

SUSAN DELMONTE
GRAND ISLAND, NEW YORK

TAPENADE

1 cup pitted kalamata olives

1 cup pitted domestic ripe olives

3 tablespoons grated pecorino-Romano cheese

1 tablespoon pureed garlic

1 teaspoon finely minced fresh basil

1/4 cup olive oil

CRISPS

4 (7-inch) pita breads

1/2 cup olive oil

2 tablespoons chopped fresh oregano

1 cup (4 oz.) grated pecorino-Romano cheese

❶ In food processor, combine olives, cheese, garlic, basil and olive oil; process until finely chopped. Pour olive mixture into medium bowl. Refrigerate, covered, 2 hours.

❷ Heat oven to 400°F.

❸ Cut each round pita bread into 8 wedges; brush each wedge with olive oil. Sprinkle each with oregano and cheese. Arrange wedges on baking sheet. Bake 10 minutes or until golden brown. Remove from baking sheet; cool. Serve with tapenade.

10 servings.

CHEESE WAFERS

SHEILA HUSBERG
SCOTTSDALE, ARIZONA

1 lb. grated cheddar cheese

3 cups all-purpose flour

1 cup butter, softened

1 teaspoon salt

1/4 teaspoon cayenne pepper

1 cup chopped pecans, if desired

❶ In large bowl, beat cheese, flour, butter, salt and cayenne at medium speed until well combined. Mix in pecans. Divide dough into thirds. Form each third into smooth logs 1 1/2 inches thick. Wrap tightly in parchment paper; refrigerate at least 1 hour or until firm.

❷ Heat oven to 325°F. Remove paper. Cut dough into 1 1/2-inch slices. Arrange slices 1 1/2 inches apart on baking sheets. Bake 15 to 18 minutes or until golden brown. Transfer to paper towels; cool completely. Store in airtight container.

40 servings.

TOMATO-BASIL PIE

BETSY GAYNER
CAMP HILL, PENNSYLVANIA

1 (9-inch) unbaked pie shell

1 1/2 cups (6 oz.) shredded mozzarella cheese

5 plum tomatoes, sliced

1/2 cup loosely packed fresh basil

2 garlic cloves, chopped

1/2 cup mayonnaise

1/2 cup (2 oz.) grated Parmesan cheese

1/8 teaspoon ground white pepper

❶ In 9-inch pie plate, bake pie shell according to package directions. Sprinkle 1/2 cup of the mozzarella cheese over crust while it is still warm. Let cool.

❷ Heat oven to 375°F. Arrange tomatoes over cheese. In small bowl, combine basil and garlic; mix well. Sprinkle over tomatoes. Combine remaining 1 cup mozzarella, mayonnaise, Parmesan and pepper; mix well. Spread over top of pie.

❸ Bake 35 to 40 minutes or until top is golden and bubbly. Serve warm.

12 servings.

EASY VEGGIE PIZZA

JULIE OSTROM
CHIPPEWA FALLS, WISCONSIN

1 cup spinach dip
1 (10-oz.) thin crust Italian bread shell
1 cup chopped fresh broccoli
⅓ cup sliced green onions
1 cup chopped seeded tomato
1 cup (4 oz.) shredded sharp cheddar cheese
½ cup sliced ripe olives

❶ Spread spinach dip evenly over bread shell to within ½ inch of edge. Top evenly with broccoli, onions, tomato, cheese and olives. Cut into squares before serving.

10 servings.

TORTILLA SNACK STRIPS

CHRIS McBEE
XENIA, OHIO

2 tablespoons margarine, melted
6 (8-inch) flour tortillas
½ teaspoon ground cumin
½ teaspoon garlic powder
½ teaspoon onion powder
Dash of cayenne pepper

❶ Heat oven to 400°F.

❷ Brush margarine over 1 side of each tortilla. In small bowl, combine cumin, garlic powder, onion powder and cayenne; lightly sprinkle cumin mixture evenly over each tortilla.

❸ Make 2 stacks of tortillas. Using a serrated knife, cut each stack into 9 thin strips. Arrange stacks on 15x10x1-inch baking pan. Bake 8 to 10 minutes. Serve warm.

12 servings.

LEMON-PEPPER BISCOTTI

ANN NACE
PERKASIE, PENNSYLVANIA

2¼ cups all-purpose flour
⅓ cup freshly grated Parmesan cheese
2 tablespoons freshly ground pepper
1½ teaspoons baking powder
½ teaspoon salt
½ cup butter, softened
2½ tablespoons sugar
2 eggs
2 tablespoons chopped fresh parsley
3 teaspoons grated lemon peel

❶ Heat oven to 325°F. Lightly grease baking sheet.

❷ In medium bowl, combine flour, cheese, pepper, baking powder and salt. In another medium bowl, beat butter and sugar at high speed until creamy. Beat in eggs, parsley and lemon peel until combined. Reduce speed to low; beat in flour mixture until dough forms. Divide dough in half. With floured hands, shape each piece into 12-inch log. Arrange logs on baking sheet; bake 25 minutes.

❸ Remove logs from oven; cool 5 minutes. Cut each log diagonally into slices 1½ inches thick. Arrange slices on baking sheet, cut side down. Bake an additional 10 minutes per side or until golden. Cool on wire racks.

12 servings.

TOASTED RAVIOLI

DEBBIE BYRNE
CLINTON, CONNECTICUT

1 (9-oz.) pkg. cheese-filled ravioli
¾ cup dry bread crumbs
2 tablespoons freshly grated Parmesan cheese
1 teaspoon dried basil
1 teaspoon dried oregano
¼ teaspoon freshly ground pepper
2 egg whites
1 (26-oz.) jar pasta sauce
Olive oil cooking spray

❶ Cook ravioli according to package directions, omitting salt. Rinse under cold running water until ravioli are cool; drain well.

❷ Heat oven to 375°F. Spray large baking sheet with nonstick cooking spray.

❸ In medium bowl, combine bread crumbs, cheese, basil, oregano and pepper; mix well.

❹ In shallow dish, beat egg whites at low speed. Dip ravioli, a few at a time, in egg whites; roll in crumb mixture, tossing to coat evenly. Arrange ravioli on baking sheet; spray each with olive oil cooking spray.

❺ Bake 12 to 14 minutes or until crisp. Meanwhile, heat sauce; serve with ravioli.

8 servings.

PARMESAN-CHIVE LACE APPETIZERS

JULIE OSTROM
CHIPPEWA FALLS, WISCONSIN

¾ cup (3 oz.) freshly grated Parmesan cheese
1 tablespoon chopped fresh parsley
1 tablespoon chopped fresh chives
¼ teaspoon paprika

❶ Heat oven to 400°F.

❷ In medium bowl, combine cheese, parsley, chives and paprika; mix well.

❸ Spoon 1 teaspoon of cheese mixture into 2-inch circle, 2 inches apart onto baking sheet. Bake 1 to 2 minutes or until very lightly browned. Remove from oven; cool 1 minute. Transfer appetizers to wire rack; cool an additional 5 minutes.

12 servings.

REUBEN PIZZA

MRS. WILLIAM LEHMAN
GALENA, ILLINOIS

1 (12-inch) unbaked Italian pie shell
1 (8-oz.) bottle Thousand Island dressing
16 oz. corned beef, shredded
1 (14-oz.) can sauerkraut, drained
1 teaspoon caraway seeds, if desired
1 cup (4 oz.) shredded Swiss cheese
1 cup (4 oz.) shredded mozzarella cheese

❶ Heat oven to 350°F.

❷ Place pie shell on 12-inch pizza pan. Spread dressing evenly over crust. Layer corned beef, sauerkraut and caraway seeds evenly over dressing. Sprinkle with cheeses.

❸ Bake 30 minutes or until thoroughly heated and cheeses are melted. Cut into squares. Serve warm.

12 servings.

COLORFUL CRAB APPETIZER PIZZA

DIANE CARON
WINTERSET, IOWA

1 (8-oz.) can refrigerated crescent roll dough

1 (8-oz.) pkg. cream cheese, softened

1 1/2 cups coarsely chopped fresh spinach

1 green onion, thinly sliced

1 1/2 teaspoons minced fresh dill or 1/2 teaspoon dried dill

1 teaspoon grated lemon peel

1/2 teaspoon fresh lemon juice

1/8 teaspoon freshly ground pepper

1 1/4 cups canned lump crabmeat, drained, flaked

1/4 cup chopped ripe olives

❶ Heat oven to 350°F. Spray 12-inch pizza pan with nonstick cooking spray.

❷ Unroll crescent roll dough and place on pan. Flatten dough, sealing seams and perforations. Bake 8 to 10 minutes or until lightly browned; cool.

❸ In small bowl, beat cream cheese at medium speed until smooth. Stir in 1 cup of the spinach, onion, dill, 1/2 teaspoon of the lemon peel, lemon juice and pepper; mix well. Spread mixture over crust. Top with crab, olives, remaining 1/2 cup spinach and remaining 1/2 teaspoon lemon peel. Cut into 1-inch squares.

8 to 10 servings.

MELT-IN-YOUR-MOUTH CHEESE STICKS

GWEN CAMPBELL
STERLING, VIRGINIA

1/2 cup butter, softened

3/4 cup all-purpose flour

2 tablespoons ice water

2 tablespoons grated Monterey Jack cheese

2 tablespoons grated sharp cheddar cheese

2 tablespoons grated Swiss cheese

1/4 teaspoon salt

1 tablespoon sesame seeds

1 tablespoon poppy seeds

❶ Heat oven to 350°F. Cover baking sheet with aluminum foil.

❷ In large bowl, beat butter until light and creamy. Stir in flour. Add water, cheeses and salt; stir until soft dough forms. Using cookie press, pipe dough onto baking sheet in 40 (2-inch) lines or break off 40 small balls of dough and roll into 2-inch ropes.

❸ Arrange sticks on baking sheet. Sprinkle with seeds. Bake 15 minutes or until golden and crispy. Remove from oven; cool on baking sheet.

12 servings.

SAVORY PARTY BREAD

VIVIAN NIKANOW
CHICAGO, ILLINOIS

1 (1-lb.) round loaf sourdough bread

1 lb. sliced Monterey Jack cheese

1/2 cup butter, melted

1/2 cup chopped green onions

❶ Heat oven to 350°F.

❷ Cut bread in half, then crosswise without cutting through to bottom of crust. Insert cheese between cuts.

❸ In small bowl, combine butter and onions; drizzle over bread. Wrap bread in aluminum foil; place on baking sheet. Bake 15 minutes. Uncover; bake an additional 10 minutes or until cheese is melted.

8 servings.

MOZZARELLA-SALAMI HORS D'OEUVRES

CHRISANN LEWART
EASTON, PENNSYLVANIA

4 cups (1 lb.) shredded mozzarella cheese

½ lb. salami or pepperoni slices

3 eggs

3 tablespoons freshly grated Parmesan cheese

⅛ teaspoon freshly ground pepper

1 (8-oz.) can refrigerated crescent roll dough

❶ Heat oven to 325°F. Spray 13x9-inch pan with nonstick cooking spray. Press rolls into bottom of pan to cover.

❷ In large bowl, combine cheese, salami, eggs, cheese and pepper; mix well. Spread mixture evenly over tops of rolls. Arrange rolls on pan. Bake 40 to 45 minutes or until lightly browned. Cut into 24 squares. Serve warm.

12 servings.

CHEESE COOKIES

CARYL ZEINER
TAMARAC, FLORIDA

½ lb. butter, softened

2 cups (8 oz.) grated cheddar cheese

2 cups all-purpose flour

2 cups puffed rice cereal

½ teaspoon salt

½ teaspoon cayenne pepper

❶ Heat oven to 375°F.

❷ In large bowl, combine butter, cheese, flour, cereal, salt and cayenne; mix well. With hands, form mixture into balls. Arrange balls on baking sheet. Flatten with fork tines.

❸ Bake 10 to 15 minutes or until lightly browned and crisp.

16 servings.

PIZZA BIANCO

MARIA BERARDUCCI
NORTH PROVIDENCE, RHODE ISLAND

1 (12-inch) unbaked Italian pie shell

1 (16-oz.) can cannellini beans, drained

1 teaspoon dried parsley

1 garlic clove, minced

Dash of crushed red pepper

⅛ teaspoon salt

⅛ teaspoon freshly ground pepper

½ white onion, finely chopped

4 slices Italian ham or pepperoni, if desired, chopped

½ cup olive oil

½ cup (2 oz.) shredded mozzarella cheese

¼ cup (1 oz.) freshly grated Romano cheese

❶ Spray 12-inch pizza pan with nonstick cooking spray. Press pie shell into pan.

❷ In large bowl, combine beans, parsley, garlic, red pepper, salt, pepper, onion, ham and oil; mix well. Spread bean mixture evenly over dough.

❸ Heat oven to 400°F. Bake 20 minutes or until golden. Remove from oven; sprinkle with mozzarella. Bake an additional 5 minutes or until cheese is melted. Cut into appetizer-size pieces. Sprinkle with Romano cheese.

12 servings.

ONION RYE CRACKERS & SESAME SEED STICKS

ONION RYE CRACKERS

DEANNE ROBERTS
OREM, UTAH

1½ cups all-purpose flour
½ cup rye flour
2 teaspoons instant minced onion
2 teaspoons baking powder
1 teaspoon salt
¼ cup butter, chilled, cut up
½ cup water
1 egg white
Sesame, celery or caraway seeds

❶ Heat oven to 400°F.

❷ In medium bowl, combine all-purpose flour, rye flour, onion, baking powder and salt. Cut in butter until well blended. Add water; mix well, forming a ball. Divide dough into 2 pieces. Roll each piece on lightly greased baking sheet. With small rolling pin or smooth glass, roll dough thin (12x10-inches). Dough should cover entire tray.

❸ Dust rolling pin with flour. Brush dough with egg white; sprinkle with seeds. Press in seeds with rolling pin. Cut in squares or triangles with pizza cutter or sharp knife.

❹ Bake 10 minutes or until crackers are crisp and lightly browned.

12 servings.

SESAME SEED STICKS

BARBARA ARDIS
MANNING, SOUTH CAROLINA

2 cups all-purpose flour
½ teaspoon salt
¾ cup butter, chilled, cut up
2 tablespoons ice water
1 egg white
Sesame seeds
Dash of cayenne pepper
⅛ teaspoon kosher (coarse) salt

❶ Heat oven to 325°F. Line baking sheet with parchment paper. In small bowl, sift flour and salt; cut in butter. Sprinkle dough with ice water; toss with fork until dough holds together. Roll dough out onto floured surface; cut with pizza cutter into 1x3-inch strips.

❷ Place strips on baking sheet. Brush each with egg white; sprinkle each with sesame seeds and cayenne. Bake 20 to 25 minutes or until lightly browned on bottom. Sprinkle each with salt.

12 servings.

CHEESY SNACKS

MRS. DONELDA WILDUNG
WINIFRED, MONTANA

4 cups (1 lb.) grated Monterey Jack cheese
4 cups (1 lb.) grated cheddar cheese
½ cup mayonnaise
1 (3.8-oz.) can sliced ripe olives, drained
¼ teaspoon onion salt
⅛ teaspoon garlic powder
3 tablespoons chopped onion
6 English muffins, halved

❶ Heat oven to 350°F.

❷ In large bowl, combine cheeses, mayonnaise, olives, salt, garlic powder and onion; mix well. Spread mixture evenly over each English muffin half. Arrange on baking sheet. Bake 10 to 15 minutes or until cheese is melted.

24 servings.

CHEESE-TOMATO BREAD

SARAH ROARK
ROSSVILLE, ILLINOIS

2 tablespoons margarine

1 medium onion, minced

1/2 cup sour cream

1/4 cup mayonnaise

1 cup (4 oz.) shredded cheddar cheese

3/4 teaspoon salt

1/4 teaspoon freshly ground pepper

1/4 teaspoon dried oregano

Dash of dried sage

1/3 cup milk

2 cups baking mix

3 medium tomatoes, peeled, seeded, sliced (1/4 inch thick)

1/8 teaspoon paprika

❶ Heat oven to 400°F. Spray 13x9-inch pan with nonstick cooking spray.

❷ In large skillet, melt margarine over medium heat. Add onion; sauté until tender. Remove from heat. Add sour cream, mayonnaise, cheese, salt, pepper, oregano and sage. Set aside.

❸ In medium bowl, add milk to baking mix. Turn dough out onto well-floured surface; knead dough lightly. Pat dough into bottom and up sides of pan. Arrange tomato slices over dough. Spoon sour cream mixture over tomatoes. Sprinkle with paprika. Bake 25 minutes. Let stand 10 minutes before cutting.

12 servings.

ITALIAN NACHOS

WENDY INTVELD
ST. PAUL, MINNESOTA

1 (1-lb) pkg. wonton wrappers

1 cup vegetable oil

1 (10-oz.) pkg. alfredo sauce mix

1 lb. bulk mild Italian sausage

1 green bell pepper, chopped

1 red bell pepper, chopped

1 yellow or orange bell pepper, chopped

3 green onions, coarsely chopped

Vegetable oil for frying

❶ Cut wonton wrappers into triangles.

❷ In large skillet, heat oil over medium-high heat until hot. Fry wrappers in oil, 4 or 5 pieces at a time until golden brown. Remove to paper towels; drain.

❸ Place single layer of cooked wrappers on large platter. Prepare alfredo sauce according to package directions. Pour sauce over wrappers.

❹ In another large skillet, cook sausage over medium heat until no longer pink. Drain; set aside.

❺ Sprinkle bell pepper and green onions over alfredo sauce. Top with sausage. Serve immediately.

12 servings.

BACON BUNS

DOLORES ARNETT
KENOSHA, WISCONSIN

1 lb. thick-sliced bacon, cooked, crumbled

½ cup finely chopped onions

Dash of freshly ground pepper

3 (8-oz.) cans refrigerated crescent roll dough

1 egg yolk

1 teaspoon water

❶ Heat oven to 375°F.

❷ In large skillet, cook bacon, onions and pepper over medium heat until bacon is crisp and onions and pepper are tender.

❸ Unroll crescent rolls and split triangles apart at serrated line. Place small amount of bacon mixture in center of triangle; fold together and pinch dough to seal. Place dough, seam side down on baking sheet.

❹ In small bowl, combine egg yolk and water. Brush tops of buns with egg mixture. Arrange buns on baking sheet. Bake 11 to 13 minutes or until golden brown. Cool on wire rack.

24 servings.

PARTY PIZZAS

SANDRA HOUNSOM
ST. LOUIS, MISSOURI

½ lb. bulk pork sausage

½ lb. processed cheese spread loaf

1 tablespoon ketchup

½ teaspoon Worcestershire sauce

½ teaspoon garlic salt

½ teaspoon dried oregano

1 loaf rye bread, cut into 2-inch pieces

❶ Heat oven to 375°F. In large skillet, cook sausage over medium heat until no longer pink; drain.

❷ In large microwave-safe bowl, melt cheese at Low power. Add sausage, ketchup, Worcestershire sauce, garlic salt and oregano; stir to combine. Spread mixture evenly onto bread slices.

❸ Place slices on baking sheets. Bake 5 minutes.

12 servings.

VEGETABLE PIZZA

CHRIS McBEE
XENIA, OHIO

3 (8-oz.) cans reduced-fat refrigerated crescent roll dough

2 (8-oz.) pkg. reduced-fat cream cheese, softened

⅔ cup reduced-fat mayonnaise

1 tablespoon dill weed

4 tomatoes, seeded, chopped

2 cups chopped fresh broccoli

3 green onions, thinly sliced

2 cups sliced fresh mushrooms

½ medium green bell pepper, chopped

1 (2-oz.) can sliced ripe olives, drained

2 cups (8 oz.) reduced-fat shredded cheddar cheese

❶ Heat oven to 400°F. Spray 2 (15x10x1-inch) pans with nonstick cooking spray.

❷ Unroll crescent rolls and split triangles apart at serrated line. Press dough into bottom of pan, sealing seams and perforations. Bake 10 minutes or until light golden brown. Remove from oven; cool.

❸ In small bowl, blend cream cheese, mayonnaise and dill. Spread mixture evenly over crusts. Top each crust evenly with vegetables, olives and cheese. Cut into 1- or 2-inch squares. Refrigerate until ready to serve.

36 servings.

STUFFED ARTICHOKE BREAD

DARRELYN ADKISON
COLUMBIA STATION, OHIO

1 loaf Italian or French bread, halved lengthwise

1/2 cup butter

6 garlic cloves, minced

2 tablespoons sesame seeds

1 1/2 cups sour cream

2 cups (8 oz.) Monterey Jack cheese, cubed

1/4 cup (1 oz.) freshly grated Parmesan cheese

2 tablespoons dried parsley

2 teaspoons lemon pepper

1 (14-oz.) can artichokes, drained, chopped

1 cup (4 oz.) shredded sharp cheddar cheese

❶ Heat oven to 350°F. Line baking sheet with aluminum foil.

❷ Hollow out each bread half; tear bread into bite-size pieces.

❸ In large skillet, melt butter over medium heat. Add garlic; sauté until tender. Add bread pieces; toss and stir until bread absorbs butter.

❹ In large bowl, combine bread mixture, sesame seeds, sour cream, Monterey Jack and Parmesan cheeses, parsley, lemon pepper and artichokes; mix well. Evenly scoop mixture into bread halves. Sprinkle with cheddar cheese. Arrange bread halves on baking sheet. Bake 30 minutes. Slice into 2-inch pieces or cube and serve with toothpicks.

16 servings.

FOCACCIA BREAD

CHRISTINA CUTTLE
MEDFORD, MASSACHUSETTS

2 1/3 to 3 cups all-purpose flour

2 teaspoons sugar

1/4 teaspoon kosher (coarse) salt

1 (2.25-oz.) pkg. active dry yeast

1/4 cup olive oil, plus 1 tablespoon for brushing

1 cup warm water (120°F to 130°F)

1 tablespoon chopped fresh herbs (basil, rosemary, and thyme, etc.)

❶ Spray 13x9-inch pan with nonstick cooking spray. In large bowl, combine 2 1/3 cups of the flour, sugar, salt and yeast; mix well. Add 1/4 cup of the olive oil and water; beat at medium speed 3 minutes. Stir in remaining 1 1/2 to 2 cups flour until dough is soft and leaves sides of bowl. Cover and let rise 1 hour or until dough has doubled.

❷ Heat oven to 425°F.

❸ Knead dough on lightly floured surface 5 to 10 minutes or until dough is smooth and elastic. Shape dough into 8x12-inch rectangle on parchment paper-lined baking sheet. Make indentations over entire surface with fingertips. Brush dough with remaining olive oil. Sprinkle with herbs. Place bread on pan. Bake 12 to 15 minutes or until golden brown. Serve warm or cool.

8 to 10 servings.

SPICY CHEESE STRAWS

SHEONA WILLIAMS
MITCHELL, SOUTH DAKOTA

1 (17.25-oz.) pkg. frozen puff pastry sheets, thawed
1 egg, beaten
1 cup (4 oz.) freshly grated Parmesan cheese
¼ teaspoon cayenne pepper
¾ teaspoon paprika

❶ Heat oven to 375°F. Spray baking sheet with non-stick cooking spray.

❷ On floured surface, smooth pastry with rolling pin. Brush with egg.

❸ In small bowl, combine cheese, pepper and paprika. Sprinkle cheese mixture over pastry, pressing mixture in. Cut each sheet in half lengthwise; cut each half crosswise into 8 strips. Cut a 3-inch slit down center of each strip. Fold end through slit from top; fold opposite end through strip from underneath and pull through.

❹ Place on baking sheet; brush with remaining egg. Bake 20 to 25 minutes or until golden.

16 servings.

APPETIZER STROMBOLI

CHRIS McBEE
XENIA, OHIO

2 (1-lb.) loaves frozen bread dough, thawed
¼ lb. sliced ham
¼ lb. sliced pepperoni
¼ cup chopped onions
¼ cup chopped green bell peppers
1 (14-oz.) jar pizza sauce
¼ lb. sliced mozzarella cheese
¼ lb. sliced bologna
¼ lb. sliced hard salami
¼ lb. sliced Swiss cheese
1 teaspoon dried basil
1 teaspoon dried oregano
¼ teaspoon garlic powder
¼ teaspoon freshly ground pepper
1 tablespoon butter, melted

❶ Spray 15x10x1-inch baking pan with cooking spray. Let dough rise in warm place until doubled. Punch dough down. Roll loaves together into 15x12-inch rectangle. Layer ham and pepperoni lengthwise on half of the dough. Sprinkle with onions and bell peppers. Top with ¼ cup of the pizza sauce. Layer mozzarella, bologna, salami and Swiss cheese over sauce. Sprinkle with basil, oregano, garlic powder and pepper. Spread another ¼ cup of pizza sauce on top. Fold dough over the filling; seal edges. Place on baking pan.

❷ Heat oven to 375°F. Bake 30 to 35 minutes or until golden brown. Brush with melted butter. Heat remaining pizza sauce and serve with sliced stromboli.

8 to 10 servings.

PITA PIZZA

BRENDA HENDRICKX
ST. CLOUD, MINNESOTA

1 (8-oz.) pkg. cream cheese, softened
1/3 cup mayonnaise
1/4 cup chopped green onions
1/2 teaspoon dill weed
1/2 teaspoon garlic powder
1/2 teaspoon salt
6 (7-inch) pita rounds
1 1/2 cups shredded iceberg lettuce
1 1/2 cups shredded carrots
2 cups (8 oz.) shredded cheddar cheese
1 red bell pepper, diced
1 tomato, seeded, diced

❶ In medium bowl, combine cream cheese, mayonnaise, green onions, dill weed, garlic powder and salt; mix well. Spread 2 tablespoons of the mixture over each pita round. Top each pita evenly with lettuce, carrots, cheese, bell pepper and tomato. Cut pitas into 6 to 8 wedges. Serve immediately.

15 to 20 servings.

GARDEN VEGETABLE PIZZA

SHEILA SLOAN
HULL, GEORGIA

CRUST
2 cups all-purpose flour
1 cup whole wheat flour
1 (1/4-oz.) pkg. active dry yeast
1 cup warm water (120°F to 130°F)
2 teaspoons cornmeal

TOPPING
1 cup pizza sauce
1 cup chopped red bell pepper
1 cup chopped green bell pepper
1 cup sliced fresh mushrooms
1/4 cup chopped fresh basil, if desired
2 cups (8 oz.) finely shredded reduced-fat mozzarella cheese

❶ In large bowl, combine 1 cup of the all-purpose flour, 1/4 cup of the whole-wheat flour and yeast. Add warm water; beat at low speed 30 seconds, scraping sides of bowl constantly. Increase speed to high; beat an additional 3 minutes.

❷ Using a spoon, stir in remaining 3/4 cup whole-wheat flour and as much of the remaining 1 cup all-purpose flour as possible.

❸ Turn dough out onto lightly floured surface. Knead in enough of the remaining all-purpose flour to make a stiff dough that is smooth and elastic. Divide dough in half. Cover and let rest 10 minutes.

❹ Heat oven to 425°F. Lightly spray 2 (12-inch) pizza pans with nonstick cooking spray. Sprinkle each pan with 1 teaspoon cornmeal.

❺ On lightly floured surface, roll each portion of the dough into a 13-inch circle. Transfer dough to pans. Build up the edges slightly. Do not let rise. Bake 12 minutes or until lightly browned.

❻ Spread pizza sauce over top of hot crusts. Sprinkle with bell peppers, mushrooms and basil. Top with cheese. Bake 10 to 15 minutes or until cheese melts.

24 servings.

MINI PIZZAS

A.C. JOHNSON
PHILADELPHIA, PENNSYLVANIA

1 (8-oz.) can refrigerated pizza dough

3 tablespoons butter, softened

1 tablespoon chopped fresh herbs

1/2 teaspoon grated lemon peel

1 teaspoon fresh lemon juice

1 large tomato

8 stuffed green olives, sliced

4 whole baby corns

8 fresh mushrooms, sliced

4 oz. mozzarella cheese, sliced

8 ripe olives, sliced

16 fresh basil leaves

❶ Heat oven to 400°F. Line baking sheet with parchment paper.

❷ Using sharp knife, cut pizza dough into 8 pieces; roll dough into balls. Roll each ball into 4-inch circle. Arrange crusts on baking sheet. Bake, uncovered, 10 minutes. Remove crusts from oven. Top each crust with 1 tomato slice, green olive slices, 1 baby corn, mushrooms, 1 slice mozzarella and 2 ripe olive slices.

❸ In large bowl, combine butter, herbs, lemon peel and lemon juice; mix well. Arrange pizzas on baking sheet. Brush each crust with butter mixture. Bake 20 minutes or until crusts are lightly browned and cheese is melted. Garnish each with fresh basil.

8 servings.

MEXICAN SQUARES

JENNIFER KALLEN
DYER, INDIANA

2 (8-oz.) cans refrigerated crescent roll dough

1 (16-oz.) can refried beans

1 cup sour cream

2 tablespoons taco seasoning mix

1 1/2 cups (6 oz.) shredded cheddar cheese

1/2 cup sliced green onions

1/2 cup chopped green bell peppers

1 cup seeded chopped tomatoes

1/2 cup sliced ripe olives

❶ Heat oven to 375°F. Spray 15x10x1-inch baking pan with nonstick cooking spray.

❷ Separate dough into 4 long rectangles. Arrange crosswise in pan; press into bottom and 1 inch up sides to form crust. Press perforations together to seal. Bake 14 to 19 minutes or until golden brown; cool.

❸ Spread beans evenly over crust within 1/2 inch of edge. In small bowl, combine sour cream and taco seasoning; mix well. Spread sour cream mixture evenly over beans. Spread cheese, onions, bell peppers, tomatoes and olives evenly over sour cream mixture. Refrigerate, covered, 1 hour. Cut into squares.

12 servings.

SAVORY SHRIMP AND ITALIAN CHEESE APPETIZERS

MARY HILDEBRAND
RHINELANDER, WISCONSIN

1 (8-oz.) can refrigerated crescent roll dough

1 (8-oz.) pkg. mixed Italian shredded cheeses

1 cup minced shelled, deveined cooked medium shrimp

1 tablespoon chopped green onions

1 egg

1 tablespoon brandy or white wine, if desired

❶ Heat oven to 350°F.

❷ Roll out and separate crescent rolls, pinching each perforation together to make a rectangle of dough.

❸ In large bowl, combine cheese, shrimp, onions, egg and wine; mix well. Spread mixture evenly over dough; roll up tightly, jelly-roll style. Cut roll into 1-inch slices. Arrange slices in 13x9-inch pan.

❹ Bake 10 to 12 minutes or until lightly browned. Remove from oven; cool slightly.

8 servings.

CHEESY PEANUT STRIPS

VICKI WILLIAMSON
BELLINGHAM, WASHINGTON

1 (8-oz.) pkg. corn muffin mix

1 egg

⅓ cup milk

½ cup chopped salted peanuts

1½ cups (6 oz.) shredded cheddar cheese

1 (2-oz.) jar diced pimientos, drained

❶ Heat oven to 375°F.

❷ Prepare corn muffin mix according to package directions, adding egg and milk. Stir all but 2 tablespoons peanuts into corn muffin mixture. Spread mixture evenly onto 13x9-inch pan.

❸ In medium bowl, combine cheese with pimientos; sprinkle over corn muffin mixture. Sprinkle reserved peanuts over top.

❹ Bake 20 minutes or until lightly browned. Cut into strips and serve warm.

12 servings.

Sips
&
Nibbles

ITALIAN-STYLE NIBBLE MIX

SANDRA HOUNSOM
ST. LOUIS, MISSOURI

1/4 cup popped popcorn

2 cups bite-sized shredded wheat squares

2 cups puffed oat cereal

2 tablespoons butter, melted

1/4 cup (1 oz.) freshly grated Parmesan cheese

1 tablespoon dry Italian salad dressing mix

❶ Heat oven to 300°F.

❷ In 13x9-inch pan, combine popcorn, wheat squares and puffed oat cereal. Bake 5 minutes. Remove from oven. Drizzle with melted butter.

❸ In medium bowl, combine Parmesan and salad dressing mix; sprinkle over popcorn mixture. Stir well.

10 servings.

CHEESE BALLS WITH PINEAPPLE

CHRISTINE WOLFE
CAPE CORAL, FLORIDA

8 iceberg lettuce leaves

8 pineapple slices

1 (8-oz.) pkg. cream cheese

2 cups finely chopped macadamia nuts

❶ Place 1 lettuce leaf on each of 8 individual salad plates. Place 1 pineapple slice on each lettuce leaf.

❷ Place cream cheese block on cutting board; cut 8 equal squares. Roll each square into a ball, then roll each ball in nuts. Place 1 ball on each pineapple slice. Sprinkle any remaining macadamia nuts over salads. Refrigerate until ready to serve.

8 servings.

PASSION POTION

CHRISANN LEWERT
EASTON, PENNSYLVANIA

3 oz. brandy

3 oz. grenadine

4 1/2 oz. cherry brandy

12 oz. fresh orange juice

12 oz. fresh lemon juice

❶ In blender, combine brandy, grenadine, cherry brandy, orange juice and lemon juice; blend well. Pour mixture into ice-filled glasses.

4 servings.

HONEY-GLAZED SNACK MIX

CHRIS McBEE
XENIA, OHIO

8 cups bite-size squares crisp corn and rice cereal

3 cups miniature pretzels

2 cups pecan halves

2/3 cup butter

1/2 cup honey

❶ Heat oven to 350°F. Spray 2 (15x10x1-inch) baking sheets with nonstick cooking spray.

❷ In large bowl, combine cereal, pretzels and pecans; set aside.

❸ In small saucepan, melt butter over medium-high heat. Stir in honey until well blended. Pour butter mixture over cereal mixture; stir to coat. Spread mixture evenly into pans. Bake 12 to 15 minutes or until mixture is lightly glazed, stirring occasionally. Cool in pans 3 minutes. Remove from pan to parchment paper; cool completely. Store in airtight container.

12 servings.

STUFFED RIPE OLIVES

LAWRENCE ASHBAUGH
TULSA, OKLAHOMA

1 (3-oz.) pkg. cream cheese, softened
1 tablespoon whipping cream
1 tablespoon grated orange peel
1 (6-oz.) can medium pitted ripe olives, drained

❶ In medium bowl, combine cream cheese, cream and orange peel; mix well. Spoon mixture into pastry bag fitted with round tip. Carefully pipe mixture into olives, filling completely. Store in refrigerator.

10 servings.

WATER CHESTNUTS

WILLY WILKINS
RICHMOND HILL, ONTARIO, CANADA

1 (10-oz.) can water chestnuts, drained
¼ cup low-sodium soy sauce
2 tablespoons brandy or dark rum
¼ cup sugar
12 thick slices maple-flavored bacon

❶ In large resealable plastic bag, combine water chestnuts, soy sauce and brandy; seal bag. Refrigerate up to 2 hours, turning often.

❷ Heat oven to 400°F. Cook bacon partially until it begins to shrink but is still soft; slice in half, crosswise. Cool to room temperature.

❸ Remove water chestnuts from marinade; discard marinade. Roll water chestnuts in sugar. Wrap bacon around water chestnuts; secure with toothpick. Arrange water chestnuts on baking sheet. Bake 10 to 15 minutes or until bacon is crisp.

8 servings.

TINY CHERRY CHEESECAKES

ALICE BLAKE
FORT STEWART, GEORGIA

CHEESECAKES
1 cup all-purpose flour
⅓ cup sugar
¼ cup unsweetened cocoa
½ cup butter, chilled
2 tablespoons cold water

FILLING
2 (3-oz.) pkg. cream cheese, softened
¼ cup sugar
2 tablespoons milk
1 teaspoon vanilla
1 egg
1 (21-oz.) can cherry pie filling

❶ Heat oven to 325°F. Spray 24 (1¾-inch) miniature muffin cups with nonstick cooking spray.

❷ In small bowl, combine flour, sugar and cocoa. Cut in butter until mixture crumbles. Gradually add water, tossing with fork until dough forms a ball. With hands, shape mixture into 24 balls. Press dough into bottom and up sides of each muffin cup.

❸ In medium bowl, beat cream cheese and sugar at medium speed until smooth. Beat in milk and vanilla. Add egg; beat at low speed just until combined. Spoon about 1 tablespoonful egg mixture over cocoa crust in each cup.

❹ Bake 15 to 18 minutes or until set. Cool on wire rack 30 minutes. Carefully remove from pans to cool completely. Top with pie filling. Store in refrigerator.

12 servings.

GREEK-STYLE OLIVES & LEMON-GARLIC OLIVES

GREEK-STYLE OLIVES

VIVIAN NIKANOW
CHICAGO, ILLINOIS

1 (6-oz.) can pitted ripe olives, drained, rinsed
¼ cup fresh lemon juice
2 slices lemon
2 whole garlic cloves
1 teaspoon dried oregano, crushed
¼ cup olive oil

❶ In airtight container, combine olives, lemon juice, lemon slices, garlic and oregano. Let olives stand at room temperature, covered for 2 days; stir occasionally.

❷ Pour olive oil over olives until completely covered. Cover container with airtight lid. Refrigerate olive mixture 2 days. Remove lemon slices. Bring to room temperature before serving. Or, if desired, refrigerate, covered, up to 2 weeks. Drain before serving.

6 servings.

LEMON-GARLIC OLIVES

VIVIAN NIKANOW
CHICAGO, ILLINOIS

1 (10-oz.) jar pimiento-stuffed olives, drained, juice reserved
4 fresh oregano sprigs
3 garlic cloves, minced
2 slices lemon
10 whole black peppercorns
3 tablespoons fresh lemon juice

❶ In olive jar, layer olives, oregano, garlic, lemon slices and peppercorns; repeat forming 2 layers.

❷ Pour lemon juice into jar; add enough reserved olive juice to fill jar. Refrigerate, covered, at least 8 hours but no more than 2 weeks.

8 servings.

CIDER NOG

FANNIE KLINE
MILLERSBURG, OHIO

2 cups half-and-half
1 cup milk
1 cup apple cider
2 eggs, beaten
½ cup sugar
⅛ teaspoon salt
⅛ teaspoon nutmeg
¼ teaspoon cinnamon
½ cup bourbon, if desired
½ cup whipped cream

❶ In large saucepan, whisk together half-and-half, milk, cider, eggs, sugar, salt, nutmeg and cinnamon. Cook over low heat until mixture thickens. Stir in bourbon. Serve nog in glass mugs. Garnish with whipped cream and dash of nutmeg or cinnamon.

6 servings.

MULLED WINE

PEGI LEE
PRIOR LAKE, MINNESOTA

SPICES
2 cinnamon sticks
6 whole cloves
6 allspice berries
Peel from 1 lemon

WINE
1 (750-ml) bottle red wine
3 tablespoons sugar
1 cup port wine

GARNISH
1 lemon, sliced
6 cinnamon sticks

❶ Tie 2 cinnamon sticks, cloves, berries and lemon peel in 6-inch square piece of cheesecloth with kitchen string. In medium saucepan, simmer spice package with wine, sugar and port wine 15 minutes. Remove spice bag.

❷ Serve wine in mugs garnished with lemon slices and cinnamon sticks.

6 servings.

SPICED BRANDY NUTS

VIRGINA SENDEK
HUNTINGTON, WEST VIRGINIA

1 lb. pecan halves
1 tablespoon cinnamon*
½ teaspoon ground allspice*
¼ teaspoon nutmeg*
¼ teaspoon ground cloves*
¼ teaspoon ground ginger*
3 oz. brandy reduced to 3 tablespoons
½ cup sugar
½ teaspoon angostura bitters
1 tablespoon Worcestershire sauce
1 tablespoon corn oil
½ teaspoon salt

❶ Heat oven to 350°F. Blanch pecans 1 minute in boiling water; drain. In small bowl, combine cinnamon, allspice, nutmeg, cloves and ginger; mix well. Set aside.

❷ In large bowl, combine reduced brandy, sugar, bitters, Worcestershire sauce and corn oil. Place hot pecans into brandy mixture. Let stand 10 minutes; spread on baking sheet. Bake 30 to 60 minutes, stirring every 10 minutes until nuts are crisp and lightly browned and liquid has evaporated.

❸ Remove pecans from oven; pour into medium bowl. Sprinkle cinnamon mixture over pecans while tossing. Turn nuts out in single layer onto parchment paper to cool.

TIP *You can use 2 tablespoons apple pie spice in place of the cinnamon, allspice, nutmeg, cloves and ginger.

16 servings.

PARTY CRACKERS

CARROL FLETCHER
GULFPORT, MASSACHUSETTS

1⅓ cups corn oil
2 (1-oz.) envelopes ranch dressing mix (not buttermilk)
4 teaspoons dill weed
2 (11-oz.) pkg. oyster crackers

❶ In 2-cup glass measuring cup, combine oil, ranch dressing mix and dill weed; mix well. Place crackers in large bowl. Pour liquid over crackers, mixing gently until oil is absorbed. Place crackers in resealable plastic bag; seal bag. Store in refrigerator up to 6 weeks.

24 servings.

CINNAMON 'N APPLE WAFERS

CHRISANN LEWERT
EASTON, PENNSYLVANIA

½ cup sugar
½ teaspoon cinnamon
¼ teaspoon nutmeg
1 small red apple, thinly sliced
1 small green apple, thinly sliced
28 shredded whole-wheat wafer crackers
10 oz. sharp white natural cheddar cheese, thinly sliced

❶ Heat oven to 350°F.

❷ In large bowl, combine sugar, cinnamon and nutmeg; mix well. Stir in apple slices; toss to coat. Place wafers on baking sheet; top each with 1 cheese slice and 2 apple slices.

❸ Bake 4 to 5 minutes or until cheese is melted. Serve warm.

12 servings.

OLIVE-FILLED CHEESE BALLS

ELIZABETH SEIBERT
KATONAH, NEW YORK

1 cup (4 oz.) shredded sharp cheddar cheese

2 tablespoons butter, softened

1/2 cup all-purpose flour

Dash of cayenne pepper

25 medium stuffed green or pitted ripe olives

❶ Heat oven to 400°F.

❷ In medium bowl, beat cheese and butter at medium speed until well blended and creamy. Stir in flour and cayenne. Roll dough into 1-inch balls; wrap dough ball around each olive.

❸ Arrange olive balls 1 inch apart on baking sheet. Bake 15 to 20 minutes.

25 servings.

WHITE SANGRIA

PEGI LEE
PRIOR LAKE, MINNESOTA

1 (750-ml) bottle dry white wine

1/4 cup peach brandy

1/4 cup superfine sugar

1 peach, thinly sliced

1 orange, thinly sliced

1 cup halved green grapes

1 1/2 cups sparkling water

❶ In large pitcher, combine wine, brandy and sugar; stir to dissolve sugar. Add sliced fruits; refrigerate, covered, at least 2 hours. Stir in sparkling water before serving over ice.

6 servings.

TARRAGON EGGS

CAROLYN LYONS
BROCKTON, MASSACHUSETTS

12 jumbo hard-cooked eggs, peeled, halved lengthwise

1/2 cup butter, melted

1 cup diced cooked chicken or turkey

2 tablespoons half-and-half

4 teaspoons chopped fresh tarragon

2 teaspoons wine vinegar

1/2 teaspoon salt

1/4 teaspoon ground white pepper

Fresh tarragon leaves

Kale or butter lettuce leaves, if desired

❶ Remove egg yolk from whites; set whites aside. In blender or food processor, combine egg yolks, butter, chicken, half-and-half, tarragon, vinegar, salt and pepper. Process until mixture is smooth. (*Eggs can be made ahead to this point. Cover and refrigerate cooked egg whites and egg yolk mixture separately up to 24 hours. Assemble and serve as directed.*)

❷ Mound egg yolk mixture into 24 egg white halves. Or, spoon mixture into pastry bag; pipe into egg white halves. Garnish with tarragon leaves. Arrange on serving plate lined with kale or butter lettuce leaves. Serve cold.

24 servings.

HOT MUSTARD POPCORN

CHRIS McBEE
XENIA, OHIO

1 teaspoon dry mustard

1/2 teaspoon dried thyme

1/2 teaspoon salt

1/4 teaspoon freshly ground pepper

Dash of cayenne pepper

3 quarts freshly popped popcorn

❶ In medium bowl, combine mustard, thyme, salt, ground pepper and cayenne pepper; mix well. Place popcorn in large bowl; sprinkle with mustard seasoning and toss.

12 servings.

SUGARED NUTS

**VIVIAN NIKANOW
CHICAGO, ILLINOIS**

2 egg whites

1 cup sugar

½ stick unsalted butter, melted

1 lb. shelled nuts

❶ Heat oven to 325°F. Line baking sheet with aluminum foil.

❷ In large bowl, beat egg whites until stiff peaks form. Beat in sugar and butter until well blended. Add nuts; stir until nuts are covered with egg white mixture. Pour nuts on baking sheet, spreading to cover bottom.

❸ Bake 30 to 40 minutes, stirring every 15 minutes, until golden brown. Remove from oven; cool in pan. Store in airtight container.

16 servings.

RANCH PRETZELS

**PAMELA THOMPSON
IPSWICH, MASSACHUSETTS**

1 (20-oz.) pkg. pretzels

1 (1-oz.) envelope ranch salad dressing mix

¾ cup vegetable oil

1½ teaspoons dill weed

1½ teaspoons garlic powder

❶ Heat oven to 200°F.

❷ Break pretzels into bite-size pieces; place in large bowl.

❸ In medium bowl, combine dressing mix, oil, dill weed and garlic powder; mix well. Pour mixture over pretzels; stir to coat. Arrange pretzels on 15x10x1-inch baking sheet. Bake 1 hour, stirring every 15 minutes.

12 servings.

CARAMEL CORN

**ROBERT MILLER
MIDDLETOWN, PENNSYLVANIA**

1 cup unpopped popcorn

1 cup packed brown sugar

1 stick butter

¼ cup white corn syrup

¼ teaspoon salt

¼ teaspoon vanilla

¼ teaspoon baking soda

⅛ teaspoon cream of tartar

❶ Heat oven to 250°F. Spray 2 (15x10x1-inch) baking sheets with nonstick cooking spray.

❷ Cook popcorn according to package directions; remove unpopped kernels. Place popcorn on baking sheets.

❸ In medium saucepan, bring brown sugar, butter, corn syrup and salt to a boil over medium-high heat; boil 5 minutes. Gradually stir in vanilla, baking soda and cream of tartar. Pour mixture over popcorn until evenly coated.

❹ Bake 1 hour, stirring every 15 minutes. Spread caramel corn on foil or parchment paper to cool.

24 servings.

SUGARED NUTS, RANCH PRETZELS & CARAMEL CORN

ICED LEMON BEVERAGE & MELONADE

ICED MELON BEVERAGE

VIANEY HERNANDEZ
VAN NUYS, CALIFORNIA

3 cups chopped honeydew melon
1 tablespoon fresh lime juice
3 tablespoons clover honey
12 ice cubes
Assorted fresh fruit
Mint leaves

❶ In blender, puree melon with lime juice and honey until smooth. Crush ice by hand or in electric crusher.

❷ To serve, fill tall glasses with crushed ice, pour melon mixture over ice; stir well. Garnish with fruit and mint.

4 servings.

MELONADE

CHRISANN LEWART
EASTON, PENNSYLVANIA

4 cups chopped watermelon
¼ cup sugar
3 tablespoons fresh lemon juice
1 liter lemon-lime carbonated beverage
1 cup lime sherbet

❶ Place half of the chopped watermelon pieces in blender; cover and blend on low speed 30 seconds or until smooth. Pour mixture into pitcher. Repeat with remaining watermelon. Gradually stir in sugar and lemon juice. Refrigerate, covered, 2 hours or until chilled.

❷ To serve, pour ⅓ cup watermelon mixture into tall glass. Fill with lemon-lime beverage; top with 1 scoop sherbet, if desired.

12 servings.

PEPPER NUTS

CHRIS McBEE
XENIA, OHIO

2 (6-oz.) cans whole natural almonds
3 tablespoons margarine
3 tablespoons Worcestershire sauce
1 teaspoon salt
1 teaspoon chili powder
½ teaspoon garlic powder
⅛ teaspoon ground white pepper
⅛ teaspoon cayenne pepper
⅛ teaspoon freshly ground pepper

❶ Heat oven to 350°F. Place almonds in medium bowl.

❷ In small skillet, melt margarine over medium-high heat. Stir in Worcestershire sauce, salt, chili powder, garlic powder, white pepper, cayenne pepper and ground pepper; cook 1 minute. Remove skillet from heat. Pour Worcestershire mixture over almonds; stir well. Let stand 30 minutes. Arrange almonds in single layer on baking sheet. Bake 35 minutes, stirring frequently. Cool completely.

8 servings.

SPIKED MINT LEMONADE

PEGI LEE
PRIOR LAKE, MINNESOTA

1 cup packed fresh mint leaves
1 cup superfine sugar
1 cup fresh lemon juice
1 cup vodka
4 cups sparkling water

❶ Crush mint leaves using mortar and pestle. In medium bowl, combine mint, sugar, lemon juice and vodka; mix well. Refrigerate, covered, 2 to 24 hours.

❷ Pour mixture through strainer; discard mint. Pour mixture into clean pitcher; stir in sparkling water. Serve over crushed ice. Garnish with mint and lemon, if desired.

6 servings.

THREE-HERBED POPCORN

CHRIS McBEE
XENIA, OHIO

6 quarts (24 cups) popped popcorn (about 1 cup unpopped kernels)

2 teaspoons salt

1/2 cup margarine

1 teaspoon dried basil

1 teaspoon dried chervil

1/2 teaspoon dried thyme

1 (12-oz.) can mixed nuts

❶ In large container, combine popcorn and salt; toss lightly to coat evenly. Set aside.

❷ In small saucepan, melt margarine over medium-high heat. Remove skillet from heat; stir in basil, chervil and thyme. Drizzle basil mixture over popcorn; toss lightly to coat evenly. Stir in nuts.

24 servings.

NO-BAKE COCOA CONFECTIONS

PENNIE GIDDINGS
SOMERS POINT, NEW JERSEY

1 1/2 cups crushed vanilla wafers (about 48)

2 tablespoons unsweetened cocoa

3/4 cup finely chopped nuts

1 1/2 tablespoons light corn syrup

1/4 cup finely chopped raisins

1/4 cup frozen orange juice concentrate, thawed

1/2 cup powdered sugar

❶ In large bowl, combine wafers, cocoa, nuts, syrup, raisins and orange juice concentrate; mix well until firm yet moist mixture forms. Roll mixture into 1-inch balls. Toss balls in powdered sugar to coat. Store between layers of parchment paper in airtight container.

12 servings.

PESTO EGGS WITH SHRIMP

PAUL PHILIPSON
REHOBOTH BEACH, DELAWARE

8 hard-cooked eggs, peeled, halved lengthwise

1/4 cup mayonnaise or salad dressing

1/4 teaspoon garlic powder

1/4 teaspoon salt

Dash of cayenne pepper

1/2 cup shelled, deveined cooked small shrimp, chopped

1 to 2 tablespoons prepared pesto

16 shelled, deveined cooked large shrimp

❶ Carefully remove egg yolks to small bowl, reserving egg white halves. Mix yolks, mayonnaise, garlic powder, salt and cayenne until fluffy. Stir in chopped shrimp.

❷ Carefully spoon yolk mixture into egg white halves. Just before serving, top each with about 1/4 teaspoon pesto and 1 whole shrimp. Serve immediately.

16 servings.

GLAZED WALNUTS

ERIN MITCHELL
STONE MOUNTAIN, GEORGIA

1/2 cup sugar

1/2 cup packed brown sugar

1/2 cup water

1 teaspoon vanilla

2 cups shelled toasted walnuts

❶ In large skillet, combine sugar, brown sugar and water. Over medium heat, stir mixture until sugars are melted. Bring to a boil. Boil until candy thermometer reaches 238°F. Carefully stir in vanilla; remove from heat. Add walnuts; stir until glazed. Spread walnuts on parchment paper; let stand until firm. Store in airtight container.

8 servings.

FRANCOISE'S DEVILED EGGS

GWEN CARTIER
NORTH HAMPTON, NEW HAMPSHIRE

12 jumbo hard-cooked eggs, peeled, halved lengthwise

2 teaspoons white vinegar

3 tablespoons finely chopped green onions

3 tablespoons finely chopped radishes

3 tablespoons finely chopped stuffed green olives

3 tablespoons finely chopped carrots

3 tablespoons finely chopped celery

3 tablespoons finely chopped green bell pepper

3 tablespoons pickle relish

1/2 cup mayonnaise

1/8 teaspoon salt

1/8 teaspoon freshly ground pepper

Dash of hot pepper sauce

Fresh parsley

Paprika

❶ Remove egg yolk from egg whites; set whites aside. In small bowl, mash egg yolks. Add vinegar; mix well. Set aside.

❷ In large bowl, combine onions, radishes, olives, carrots, celery, bell peppers, and relish. Add egg yolk mixture, mayonnaise, salt, pepper and hot pepper sauce; mix well.

❸ Mound egg yolk mixture evenly into 24 egg white halves. Garnish with paprika and parsley. Serve cold.

18 to 24 servings.

ITALIAN ANTIPASTO PLATTER

GWEN CAMPBELL
STERLING, VIRGINIA

8 thin slices Italian salami

8 thin slices prosciutto

8 anchovy fillets

2 celery hearts, cut into fourths lengthwise

1 (9-oz.) can tuna in oil, oil reserved

10 green pimiento-stuffed olives

10 pitted ripe olives

3 teaspoons capers

8 artichoke hearts

1 (2-oz.) jar pimientos

8 slices tomato

1 small green bell pepper, seeded, sliced into thin wedges

1 red bell pepper, seeded, sliced into thin wedges

1 large loaf crusty Italian bread

Butter

Assorted cheeses

Assorted fruits

❶ On large oval platter, decoratively arrange salami, prosciutto, anchovy fillets, celery, tuna, green olives, ripe olives, capers, artichoke hearts, pimientos, tomatoes and bell peppers; drizzle with reserved tuna oil. Place bread and butter on separate plate. Arrange another platter with assorted cheeses and fruits such as figs, sliced melons, peaches, bananas and apples goes well with the antipasto platter.

8 servings.

Spreads,
Mousses
& Pâtés

CHICKEN CHEESE BALLS

ANN NACE
PERKASIE, PENNSYLVANIA

1 cup seedless green grapes, halved

2 (8-oz.) pkg. cream cheese

2 (5-oz.) cans cooked shredded chicken, drained

4 green onions, finely chopped

2 tablespoons sour cream

½ teaspoon curry powder

1 teaspoon seasoned salt

1 red bell pepper, thinly sliced

Curry powder

❶ Reserve a few grapes for garnish.

❷ In large bowl, combine grapes, cream cheese, chicken, green onions, sour cream, curry powder and salt; stir until well blended. Divide mixture in half; shape each half into a ball. Cover with plastic wrap; refrigerate 8 hours or overnight to allow flavors to blend.

❸ Garnish cheese balls with grapes, bell pepper slices; sprinkle with curry powder. Serve with crackers, if desired.

16 servings.

CRAB SPREAD

JANICE POGOZELSKI
CLEVELAND, OHIO

1 (8-oz.) pkg. cream cheese, softened

1 (7-oz.) can lump crabmeat, drained, flaked

1 red bell pepper, chopped

1 large green onion, thinly sliced

1 tablespoon grated lemon peel

1 tablespoon fresh lemon juice

1 teaspoon Worcestershire sauce

¼ teaspoon hot pepper sauce

¼ teaspoon freshly ground pepper

¼ teaspoon freshly ground sea salt

❶ In large bowl, combine cream cheese, crabmeat, bell pepper, green onion, lemon peel, lemon juice, Worcestershire sauce, hot pepper sauce, pepper and salt; mix well. Refrigerate, covered, until ready to serve. Serve with crackers, if desired.

12 servings.

SIMPLE AND WONDERFUL

MICHELLE GOERGER
ALEXANDRIA, VIRGINIA

1 (8-oz.) round Brie cheese

1 (10-oz.) jar raspberry jam

1 loaf French bread, sliced

❶ Heat oven to 400°F. Place cheese in 1-quart casserole. Bake 10 minutes or until thoroughly melted. Remove from oven. Spread jam over serving platter. Spread hot cheese over jam. Top bread with cheese and jam mixture.

8 servings.

ITALIAN CHEESE LOAF

TAMI ZYLKA
BLUE BELL, PENNSYLVANIA

PESTO
1 cup fresh basil leaves
1 cup (4 oz.) freshly grated Parmesan cheese
½ cup olive oil
2 garlic cloves

GARLIC CREAM CHEESE
1 (8-oz.) pkg. cream cheese
¼ cup butter
1 garlic clove
⅛ teaspoon freshly ground pepper
¼ cup shelled pistachios, chopped

CRUST
1 to 1½ lb. thinly sliced provolone cheese
½ cup sun-dried tomato pesto

❶ In blender, combine basil, Parmesan cheese, oil and 2 garlic cloves; process until smooth.

❷ In large bowl, combine cream cheese, butter, 1 garlic clove, pepper and pistachios; mix well.

❸ Line 9-inch pie plate with damp cheesecloth. Layer provolone cheese slices over bottom and up sides of pan. Add half of the pesto mixture over cheese. Add another layer of cheese slices, followed by half of the sun-dried tomato pesto. Spread cream cheese mixture over pesto layer. Add remaining half of sun-dried tomato pesto followed by a layer of cheese. Spread with remaining basil pesto and another layer of cheese. Cover with cheesecloth; press loaf together firmly.

❹ Refrigerate, covered, 24 to 28 hours. Remove loaf from pan onto serving platter. Serve at room temperature. Serve with crackers, if desired.

12 servings.

LOW-FAT GARDEN VEGETABLE SPREAD

CAROL HAWLEY
FREDERICK, MARYLAND

1 (8-oz.) container plain low-fat yogurt
2 tablespoons shredded carrots
2 tablespoons finely chopped radishes
1 tablespoon chopped green onions
⅛ teaspoon salt
Dash of garlic powder

❶ Spoon yogurt into strainer lined with coffee filter or cheesecloth. Place strainer over bowl. Cover with plastic wrap and refrigerate. Allow to drain overnight. Discard liquid.

❷ In small bowl, combine yogurt, carrots, radishes, green onions, salt and garlic powder; mix well. Refrigerate, covered, at least 2 hours or up to 12 hours. Serve with crackers or raw vegetables, if desired.

8 servings.

CHRISTMAS SNOWBALL

CHARLOTTE WARD
HILTON HEAD ISLAND, SOUTH CAROLINA

1 (8-oz.) pkg. cream cheese, softened
1 (8-oz.) can crushed pineapple, drained
¼ jar chutney, finely chopped
1 (7-oz.) can chopped coconut
Fresh baby spinach
Fresh strawberries
Crackers

❶ In large bowl, combine cream cheese, pineapple and chutney; mix well. With hands, form mixture into a ball. Roll ball in coconut to cover. Refrigerate, covered, 4 to 6 hours or until firm.

❷ Place bed of spinach on serving platter. Place ball in the center of the platter. Garnish with strawberries, placing one strawberry on top of cheese ball. Surround with crackers.

8 to 10 servings.

DILL HAVARTI-BLUE CHEESE BALL

DILL HAVARTI-BLUE CHEESE BALL

MICHELLE MORRILL
PRESCOTT VALLEY, ARIZONA

1 (8-oz.) pkg. cream cheese, softened
½ cup (2 oz.) shredded dill Havarti cheese
⅓ cup crumbled blue cheese
1 tablespoon milk
¼ teaspoon dried oregano
2 green onions, finely chopped
½ cup sliced almonds, toasted

❶ In large bowl, beat cream cheese, Havarti cheese, blue cheese, milk, oregano and green onions at medium speed until well blended and fluffy. Refrigerate, covered, 2 hours. With hands, shape mixture into a ball. Roll ball in almonds to cover. Serve with crackers, if desired.

10 servings.

CREAM CHEESE AND CHUTNEY APPETIZER

PEGGY WINKWORTH
DURANGO, COLORADO

1 (12-oz.) jar chutney
1 (8-oz.) pkg. cream cheese
1 tablespoon chopped chives
1 (2-oz.) small pkg. chopped pecans

❶ In medium bowl, pour chutney over cream cheese; top with chives and pecans. Serve with wheat crackers, if desired.

10 servings.

CHICKEN LIVER SPREAD

BARBARA BRANDEL
LAKELAND, FLORIDA

1 tablespoon low-sodium soy sauce
½ lb. chicken livers, cooked, drained
¼ cup butter
½ teaspoon onion salt
½ teaspoon dry mustard
¼ teaspoon nutmeg
Dash of cayenne pepper
1 (8-oz.) can water chestnuts, drained, finely chopped
6 thick slices bacon, cooked, diced

❶ In food processor, combine soy sauce, chicken livers, butter, onion salt, mustard, nutmeg and cayenne; process until smooth. Stir in water chestnuts and bacon.

❷ Place mixture in serving dish. Refrigerate, covered, until ready to serve. Serve with crackers, if desired.

10 servings.

CHILI-CHEESE BALL

NANCY HROMADA
AFTON, NEW YORK

1 cup (4 oz.) grated sharp cheddar cheese
1 (8-oz.) pkg. cream cheese
¼ cup chopped walnuts
¼ teaspoon garlic powder
2 tablespoons chili powder

❶ In medium bowl, combine cheeses, walnuts and garlic powder; mix well. With hands, shape mixture into a ball. Roll ball in chili powder to cover. Wrap balls in plastic wrap. Store in refrigerator.

8 servings.

SIMPLE OLIVE SPREAD

PEGGY KREJCI
LOUDON, TENNESSEE

1 (8-oz.) pkg. reduced-fat cream cheese
¾ cup green stuffed olives, chopped
Dash of hot pepper sauce
¼ to ½ cup reduced-fat sour cream

❶ Using fork, stir together cream cheese and olives, adding enough sour cream to make creamy spread. Spoon mixture into serving bowl. Refrigerate, covered, until firm. Remove spread from refrigerator 15 minutes before serving. Serve with crackers and toasted French rounds, if desired.

10 servings.

SALMON SALAD OR SPREAD

BONITA WATTS
TULSA, OKLAHOMA

6 oz. cooked salmon, broken into small pieces
3 hard-cooked eggs, peeled, diced
½ cup reduced-fat mayonnaise
¼ cup sweet pickle relish
¼ cup chopped red or green onions
1 tablespoon capers, drained
½ teaspoon celery salt
⅛ teaspoon freshly ground pepper

❶ In large bowl, combine salmon, eggs, mayonnaise, relish, green onions, capers, celery salt and pepper; mix well. Refrigerate, covered, at least 2 hours or until chilled. Serve on crackers as an appetizer or on a lettuce leaf as a salad, if desired.

12 servings.

CRAB AND WILD MUSHROOM CHEESECAKE

TAMARA BANDSTRA
GRAND HAVEN, MICHIGAN

CRUST

1¾ cups fresh French bread crumbs
1 cup (4 oz.) freshly grated Parmesan cheese
6 tablespoons butter, melted

FILLING

1 tablespoon olive oil
1 cup chopped onions
1 cup finely chopped red bell peppers
4 cups assorted wild mushrooms, coarsely chopped (crimini, oyster and shiitake)
3 (8-oz.) pkg. cream cheese, softened, plus 1 (3-oz.) pkg.
2 teaspoons salt
1 teaspoon freshly ground pepper
4 large eggs
½ cup whipping cream
1 lb. canned lump crabmeat, drained, flaked
1 cup (4 oz.) grated smoked Gouda
½ cup chopped fresh Italian parsley

❶ Heat oven to 350°F. In medium bowl, combine bread crumbs, Parmesan cheese and melted butter; mix until well blended. Press mixture into bottom of 9-inch springform pan. Bake crust about 15 minutes or until golden brown. Cool crust while preparing filling. Maintain oven temperature.

❷ In large skillet, heat oil over medium high heat until hot. Add onions and bell peppers; sauté 2 minutes. Add mushrooms; sauté about 10 minutes or until liquid evaporates and mushrooms begin to brown. Remove skillet from heat; cool.

❸ In large bowl, beat cream cheese, salt and pepper at medium speed until mixture is fluffy. Beat in eggs, one at a time. Beat in cream. Stir in mushroom mixture, crabmeat, Gouda and parsley.

❹ Pour filling over cooled crust. Place cheesecake on baking sheet. Bake about 1½ hours or until cake puffs and browns on top but center moves slightly when pan is tapped. Transfer pan to wire rack and cool. (*Cheesecake can be prepared 1 day ahead. Cover and refrigerate.*)

❺ Run small paring knife around pan sides to loosen cheesecake. Release pan sides. Transfer cheesecake to serving platter. Serve cold or at room temperature with toasted baguette slices, if desired.

12 to 20 servings.

PERFECT PATE

DONNA FISCUS
ST. JOHN, INDIANA

1 tablespoon olive oil
1 cup chopped green onions
1 rib celery, chopped
1 lb. sliced mushrooms
1½ teaspoons dried basil
1 cup chopped walnuts
¼ teaspoon salt
¼ teaspoon freshly ground pepper
2 (8-oz.) pkg. cream cheese, softened
2 teaspoons fresh lemon juice

❶ Heat oven to 350°F. Grease 9x5-inch loaf pan.

❷ In medium skillet, heat oil over medium-high heat until hot. Add green onions, celery and mushrooms; sauté until onions are tender. Transfer mixture to food processor; process until smooth. Add basil, walnuts, salt, pepper, 8 oz. of the cream cheese and lemon juice; process until smooth.

❸ Spoon mixture into pan. Bake 1 hour or until toothpick inserted near center comes out clean. Cool pâté in pan 2 hours. Refrigerate until firm. Loosen edges with knife; invert pâté onto serving platter.

❹ In small bowl, beat remaining 8 oz. cream cheese at medium speed until smooth. Spread over pâté before serving.

16 servings.

CORNED BEEF PATE

CHARLOTTE WARD
HILTON HEAD ISLAND, SOUTH CAROLINA

1 (12-oz.) can corned beef
8 oz. braunschweiger
½ onion, finely chopped
½ cup mayonnaise
1 tablespoon vinegar
1 tablespoon Dijon mustard
1 loaf cocktail rye bread

❶ Line 3½-cup mold with plastic wrap, extending plastic wrap several inches over edges.

❷ In large bowl, flake corned beef with fork. Add braunschweiger; mix at low speed. Add onion, mayonnaise, vinegar and mustard; beat at medium speed until smooth. Place about ¾ cup of mixture into blender; blend at medium speed until smooth. Repeat with remaining mixture.

❸ Spoon mixture into mold; cover with plastic wrap. Refrigerate 24 hours. Unmold to serving plate. Serve with rye bread.

12 servings.

CUCUMBER-DILL SPREAD

CHRIS McBEE
XENIA, OHIO

1 (8-oz.) pkg. reduced-fat cream cheese, softened
2 teaspoons fresh lemon juice
2 teaspoons minced onion
½ teaspoon dill weed
¼ teaspoon prepared horseradish
⅛ teaspoon hot pepper sauce
¾ cup finely diced seeded cucumber

❶ In large bowl, beat cream cheese at medium speed until smooth. Stir in lemon juice, onion, dill, horseradish and hot pepper sauce; mix well. Fold cucumber into mixture. Refrigerate, covered, 1 hour. Serve spread with fresh vegetables or crackers, if desired.

10 servings.

SAVORY SALMON SPREAD

SHARON HUDDLE TOWERS
MANHATTAN, KANSAS

1 loaf cocktail pumpernickel rye
Olive oil cooking spray or 1 teaspoon olive oil in spray bottle
1 (8-oz.) pkg. cream cheese, softened
½ cup sour cream
5 to 6 oz. cooked salmon
3 tablespoons finely chopped red onion
3 tablespoons capers, drained
1½ teaspoons dried dill
Dash of salt
⅛ teaspoon freshly ground pepper

❶ Heat oven to 400°F. Spray baking sheet with non-stick cooking spray. Arrange bread slices in single layer on baking sheet; lightly spray with olive oil. Bake 7 minutes or until lightly toasted. Remove from oven; cool.

❷ In medium bowl, combine cream cheese, sour cream, onion, dill, salt and pepper; mix well. Carefully fold in salmon and capers. Refrigerate, covered, at least 1 hour or up to 12 hours. Spread mixture evenly over bread slices.

24 servings.

HERB-GARLIC OIL AND SUN-DRIED TOMATOES WITH BRIE

KATHLEEN MAXWELL
SYLVANIA, OHIO

1 lb. Brie cheese, chilled
4 sun-dried tomatoes packed in oil, drained, 1 tablespoon oil reserved
2 tablespoons minced fresh parsley
2 tablespoons freshly grated Parmesan cheese
1 to 2 garlic cloves, minced
2 tablespoons chopped fresh basil

❶ Remove peel from cheese with sharp knife; place cheese on serving plate.

❷ Chop tomatoes. In small bowl, combine parsley, Parmesan, tomatoes, garlic, basil and reserved oil; mix well. Spread mixture over cheese; let stand 1 hour before serving. Serves with crackers or sliced baguette, if desired.

8 to 10 servings.

CRAB MOLD

TANYA COCHRAN
FLORENCE, ALABAMA

1 lb. lump crabmeat, drained, flaked
½ cup margarine
½ cup mayonnaise
1 (8-oz.) pkg. cream cheese, softened
½ cup finely chopped pimientos
¼ cup finely chopped celery
½ teaspoon fresh lemon juice
⅛ teaspoon salt
⅛ teaspoon cayenne pepper
Lettuce leaves

❶ In medium bowl, combine crabmeat and margarine; mix well until a paste forms. Stir in mayonnaise, cream cheese, pimientos, celery, lemon juice, salt and cayenne; mix well. Cover with plastic wrap; refrigerate 2 hours.

❷ Press mixture into small bowl. Refrigerate, covered, an additional 2 to 4 hours or until firm. Arrange lettuce leaves on serving platter. Turn mold out onto center of platter. Serve with crackers, if desired.

12 servings.

HERB-GARLIC OIL AND SUN-DRIED TOMATOES WITH BRIE

HOLIDAY CHEESE BALL

DEANNE ROBERTS
OREM, UTAH

1 cup (4 oz.) grated sharp cheddar cheese

1 (8-oz.) pkg. cream cheese, softened

¼ cup finely chopped green olives with pimiento

2 tablespoons finely chopped green onion

2 tablespoons minced green bell pepper

1 teaspoon garlic powder

2 teaspoons Worcestershire sauce

1 teaspoon fresh lemon juice

½ cup chopped walnuts

1 recipe *Onion Rye Crackers* (page 91)

❶ In medium bowl, thoroughly combine cheeses, olives, green onion, bell pepper, garlic powder, Worcestershire sauce and lemon juice; with hands, form mixture into a ball. Wrap ball in plastic wrap. Refrigerate until firm. Just before serving, roll ball into chopped walnuts so that the entire surface is covered. Serve in the center of serving platter surrounded with Onion Rye Crackers.

TIP *Mixture can also be divided into holiday-shaped molds and decorated appropriately with red bell pepper slices and parsley.

10 servings.

BRIE AND PESTO

PEGGY WINKWORTH
DURANGO, COLORADO

1 (8-oz.) wheel Brie cheese

1 (3- to 5-oz.) jar pesto

❶ Heat broiler. Place cheese on baking sheet. Score top of cheese; spread pesto over top. Broil 4 inches from heat 1 minute, watching carefully, until cheese bubbles. Serve with crackers, if desired.

6 to 8 servings.

GARLIC-CHEESE SPREAD

CAROLYN LINSLEY
PITTSBURGH, PENNSYLVANIA

2 cups (8 oz.) grated Muenster cheese

3 large garlic cloves, minced

5 tablespoons mayonnaise

1 tablespoon chopped chives

⅛ teaspoon salt

❶ In medium bowl, combine cheese, garlic, mayonnaise, chives and salt; mix well. Refrigerate, covered, several hours. Serve at room temperature with thin slices of black bread, toasted rounds, French bread or crackers, if desired.

10 servings.

CHICKEN LIVER-ONION DELIGHT

CHARLOTTE WARD
HILTON HEAD ISLAND, SOUTH CAROLINA

¼ cup water

2 tablespoons dry onion soup mix

½ lb. chicken livers

1 hard-cooked egg, sliced

¼ cup mayonnaise

½ teaspoon Worcestershire sauce

3 thick slices bacon, cooked, crumbled, 1 tablespoon reserved

Watercress

1 cherry tomato

1 hard-cooked egg yolk, grated

1 loaf cocktail rye bread

❶ In medium bowl, combine water and onion soup mix; set aside. In medium pot, cover chicken livers with water. Heat to a boil. Reduce heat; simmer 8 to 10 minutes or until tender. Drain and cool.

❷ Place onion soup mixture, livers, whole hard-cooked egg, mayonnaise, Worcestershire sauce and bacon in food processor; process until smooth. Pour mixture into 2-cup mold. Refrigerate, covered, 8 hours or overnight.

❸ Unmold onto bed of watercress. Make X-cut in cherry tomato almost to bottom; open out tomato as if petals and place ⅛ teaspoon grated egg yolk in center. Top pâté with reserved bacon, grated egg yolk and cherry tomato flower. Serve with rye cocktail bread.

12 servings.

TUITY-FRUITY SPREAD

LYNDA COUNTERMAN
RICHBURG, SOUTH CAROLINA

1 (8-oz.) pkg. cream cheese

4 tablespoons orange marmalade

4 tablespoons chopped maraschino cherries

1 to 2 tablespoons Triple Sec liqueur

1 loaf sliced cinnamon bread, each slice cut into 4 squares

❶ In large bowl, combine cream cheese, marmalade, cherries and liqueur; mix well. Refrigerate, covered, until ready to serve. Transfer mixture to pastry bag fitted with large round tip. Pipe mixture onto squares of cinnamon bread.

8 servings.

SHRIMP MOLD

JEAN WETHERELL
LUDLOW, MASSACHUSETTS

1 (10.5-oz.) can condensed tomato soup

1 (1-oz.) envelope unflavored gelatin

1 (8-oz.) pkg. cream cheese

½ lb. shelled, deveined cooked small shrimp

1 cup finely chopped celery

¼ cup finely chopped onions

1 cup mayonnaise

❶ In medium pot, bring soup to a boil over medium-high heat. Sprinkle gelatin over soup; stir until dissolved. Stir in cream cheese, shrimp, celery and onions. Remove from heat; cool. Fold in mayonnaise.

❷ Pour mixture into 3-cup mold; cover with plastic wrap. Refrigerate, covered, 8 hours. Serve with crackers, if desired.

20 servings.

STILTON CHEESE TORTA

JOHN HAYES
FALLBROOK, CALIFORNIA

6 oz. sun-dried Bing cherries
1 lb. Stilton cheese
1 cup unsalted butter, softened
¼ to ½ lb. mixed pecans and walnuts
1 to 2 tablespoons olive oil

❶ Soak cherries in one cup of boiled water 5 minutes or until softened.

❷ Slice or crumble cheese into small pieces. Place cheese in food processor; process until crumbled. Add butter; process until creamy. Remove mixture to medium bowl. Wash and dry food processor bowl.

❸ Drain and chop cherries in food processor. Remove to small bowl. Wipe out food processor bowl.

❹ Place pecans and walnuts in food processor. With motor running, pour enough olive oil through feed tube as pecans are chopped to make a crumbly paste (do not blend until runny). The nut mixture should be firm, but spreadable.

❺ Invert 7½x3¾-inch loaf pan. Cover tightly with plastic wrap. Spread thin layer of the blended cheese over the bottom outside of the pan. Lift the plastic wrap off pan and lower the layer into bottom of the inside of pan. Secure plastic wrap to pan with tape.

❻ Spread the nut mixture in a layer over cheese. Spread a layer of cheese on top of the nut layer.* Cover cheese layer with layer of chopped cherries. Spread remaining cheese as final layer. Refrigerate at least one hour or until firm. To serve, unmold onto plate and serve with crackers or toasted rounds, if desired.

TIP* If the sides of your loaf pan slope, reserve more cheese for the top layer because it is wider.

8 servings.

IN-THE-PINK SPREAD

CAROLYN LINSLEY
PITTSBURGH, PENNSYLVANIA

7 to 10 sun-dried tomatoes, packed in oil, drained, 1 tablespoon oil reserved
6 oz. cream cheese, softened
2 to 3 garlic cloves, minced

❶ In blender, combine tomatoes, cream cheese, garlic and reserved oil; blend 1 minute or until smooth. Place in serving bowl. Refrigerate, covered, until firm. Serve at room temperature.

8 servings.

PARTY CHEESE BALL

JULIE MILLER
ESTHERVILLE, IOWA

2 (8-oz.) pkg. cream cheese, softened
¾ cup crumbled blue cheese
1 cup (4 oz.) shredded sharp cheddar cheese
¼ cup minced onion
1 tablespoon Worcestershire sauce
½ cup finely chopped fresh parsley

❶ In medium bowl, beat cheeses, onion and Worcestershire sauce at low speed, scraping bowl frequently, until combined. Increase speed to medium; beat until fluffy, scraping bowl frequently. Refrigerate, covered, 8 hours. With hands, shape mixture into a large ball; roll in parsley to cover. Refrigerate, covered, an additional 2 hours before serving.

12 servings.

GHERKIN-SALAMI SPREAD

**DOLORES ARNETT
KENOSHA, WISCONSIN**

2 cups (8 oz.) grated cheddar cheese

1 (3-oz.) pkg. cream cheese, softened

1/4 cup chopped pimientos, drained

3/4 cup finely chopped sweet pickles or drained pickle relish

3/4 cup finely chopped hard salami

❶ Lightly spray 1-pint mold with nonstick cooking spray.

❷ In medium bowl, combine cheese and cream cheese until well mixed. Stir in pimientos, pickles and salami; mix well. Spoon and pack mixture into mold. Refrigerate, covered, until firm. To serve, dip mold in warm water and unmold onto serving plate. Serve with assorted crackers or cocktail rye bread, if desired.

10 servings.

AUNT DONNA'S CHEESE BALLS

**DONNA GERLING
LAKE FOREST, CALIFORNIA**

1 (8-oz.) pkg. cream cheese, softened

2 cups (8 oz.) shredded sharp cheddar cheese

2 cups (8 oz.) grated Swiss or mozzarella cheese

1/2 onion, finely minced

1 tablespoon Worcestershire sauce

1/4 cup bacon-flavor bits

1/4 cup chopped fresh parsley

❶ In food processor, combine cream cheese, grated cheese, onion and Worcestershire sauce; process until smooth. Divide cheese into 3 parts. With hands, form mixture into 3 balls. Roll each ball into bacon bits and parsley. Wrap in plastic wrap. Refrigerate at least 24 hours but no more than 72 hours.

12 servings.

PINE NUT PESTO CHEESECAKE

**MARY HILDEBRAND
RHINELANDER, WISCONSIN**

CRUST

1/2 cup dry Italian bread crumbs

2 tablespoons freshly grated imported Parmesan cheese

1 tablespoon finely chopped toasted pine nuts

2 tablespoons butter, melted

FILLING

2 (8-oz.) pkg. cream cheese, softened

1 cup sour cream

1/2 cup (2 oz.) freshly grated imported Parmesan cheese

3 eggs

1/4 cup finely chopped toasted pine nuts

3 tablespoons chopped fresh basil

2 tablespoons sliced green onions

1/2 teaspoon garlic powder

1/4 teaspoon ground white pepper

1/4 teaspoon salt

Fresh basil leaves

Whole pine nuts

❶ Spray 9-inch springform pan with nonstick cooking spray. In small bowl, combine bread crumbs, 2 tablespoons Parmesan cheese, 1 tablespoon pine nuts and butter; mix well. Press mixture into bottom of pan. Set aside.

❷ Heat oven to 375°F. In large bowl, beat cream cheese at medium speed until smooth. Add sour cream and 1/2 cup Parmesan cheese; beat until smooth. Reduce speed to low, beat in eggs. Stir in 1/4 cup pine nuts, basil, green onions, garlic powder, pepper and salt; mix well. Pour filling into crust-lined pan. Bake 30 minutes or until set. Cool on wire rack. Refrigerate 3 hours or overnight. Remove sides of pan from cake. Slice thinly. Garnish with basil leaves and pine nuts.

24 servings.

SUN-DRIED TOMATO-STUFFED BRIE

MARIANNE HESTON
RALEIGH, NORTH CAROLINA

1 (7- to 8-oz.) wheel Brie cheese
2 oz. sun-dried tomatoes, soaked in olive oil, 1 tablespoon oil reserved
4 green onions (white parts only)
4 large garlic cloves
½ (17.3-oz.) pkg. frozen puff pastry sheets, thawed
Crackers

❶ Heat oven to 350°F. Cut around top of cheese, removing "lid." Set aside to use later. Scoop out about ½ cup of the cheese, making a bowl to be filled with stuffing. Reserve removed cheese for another use.

❷ In food processor, combine tomatoes, reserved olive oil, green onions and garlic; process until well blended. If too thick or dry, add a little more oil. Stuff cheese with tomato mixture; replace lid. Wrap in puff pastry, seam side down. Place on baking sheet.

❸ Bake about 30 minutes or until pastry is evenly browned. Serve hot with crackers.

8 servings.

CRAB GRASS

VEDA GODWIN
EDISTO BEACH, SOUTH CAROLINA

½ cup butter
½ medium onion, finely chopped
1 (10-oz.) pkg. frozen chopped spinach, thawed
1 (7-oz.) can lump crabmeat, drained, flaked
¾ cup (3 oz.) freshly grated Parmesan cheese

❶ Heat oven to 350°F.

❷ In medium skillet, melt butter over medium-high heat. Add onion; sauté until tender. Stir in spinach, crabmeat and Parmesan cheese; mix well. Pour mixture into 13x9-inch pan. Bake 20 minutes or until set. Serve with sesame rounds or crackers, if desired.

10 servings.

TUSCAN PATE

TAMARA BANDSTRA
GRAND HAVEN, MICHIGAN

2 (8-oz.) pkg. cream cheese, softened
½ cup butter, softened
2 teaspoons minced garlic
¼ cup finely chopped fresh basil
1 teaspoon Beau Monde seasoning
½ cup finely chopped kalamata olives
¼ cup finely chopped red bell peppers
⅛ teaspoon freshly ground pepper

❶ Line 3-cup decorative mold with plastic wrap.

❷ In medium bowl, beat cream cheese and butter at medium speed until smooth. Add garlic, basil, Beau Monde seasoning, olives, bell peppers and pepper; mix until well combined.

❸ Spoon mixture into mold; cover with plastic wrap, pressing gently to fill mold. Refrigerate several hours or overnight.

❹ To serve, gently tap out of mold. Remove plastic wrap. Arrange on decorative platter. Serve with crackers or crostini, if desired.

12 servings.

THREE-VEGETABLE PATE

CHARLOTTE G. WARD
HILTON HEAD ISLAND, SOUTH CAROLINA

SPINACH LAYER

2 (10-oz.) pkg. frozen chopped spinach, thawed, cooked, drained

2 tablespoons butter

1/2 cup chopped green onions

1/2 cup half-and-half

3 eggs, lightly beaten

1/4 cup dry stuffing mix, finely ground

1/4 cup (1 oz.) freshly grated Parmesan cheese

1/2 teaspoon salt

MUSHROOM LAYER

1 lb. fresh mushrooms

1 tablespoon fresh lemon juice

1/4 cup butter

1 cup chopped onions

2 tablespoons dry sherry

1 teaspoon salt

1/4 teaspoon freshly ground pepper

2 eggs, slightly beaten

4 tablespoons dry stuffing mix

CARROT LAYER

3 (8-oz.) cans sliced carrots, drained

2 tablespoons butter

2 tablespoons all-purpose flour

1/4 cup half-and-half

1/2 teaspoon salt

1/4 teaspoon ground ginger

1/4 teaspoon nutmeg

2 eggs, slightly beaten

Fresh dill sprigs

❶ Heat oven to 350°F. Spray 9x5-inch loaf pan with non-stick cooking spray. Line bottom and sides of pan with aluminum foil.

❷ Place spinach in large bowl. In large skillet, melt 2 tablespoons butter over medium heat. Add green onions; sauté 5 minutes or until tender. Stir in half-and-half, eggs, stuffing mix, cheese and salt. Add onion mixture to large bowl; mix well. Spoon spinach mixture into loaf pan. Smooth surface with spatula.

❸ Trim mushrooms; wipe with damp cloth. Select 8 perfect mushrooms; toss with lemon juice in medium bowl. Chop remaining mushrooms finely. In same large skillet, sauté whole mushrooms in butter 5 minutes. Arrange mushrooms in a row, lengthwise over spinach.

❹ In same large skillet, sauté chopped mushrooms and onions until very slightly browned and dry. Stir in sherry, salt and pepper. Remove from heat. Blend in eggs and stuffing mix. Spoon mixture over whole mushrooms and spinach. Smooth surface with spatula.

❺ In food processor, puree carrots until fairly smooth. In medium saucepan, melt butter over medium-high heat. Stir in flour, half-and-half, salt, ginger, nutmeg and carrots; cook, stirring constantly, until mixture comes to a boil. Remove from heat; beat in eggs, all at once. Spoon over mushroom layer.

❻ Cover pan with parchment paper, then aluminum foil. Set in larger pan; place on oven rack. Pour boiling water into larger pan to depth of 1 1/2 to 2 inches.

❼ Bake 2 hours or until pâté feels firm to the touch and knife inserted near center comes out clean. Transfer pan to wire rack. Cool 1 hour. Refrigerate, covered, overnight. Loosen around sides of pan; unmold pâté onto platter. Garnish with dill sprigs.

16 to 20 servings.

THREE-VEGETABLE PATE

GOUDA CHEESE SPREAD

EVELYN COYNE
WICKLIFFE, OHIO

1 (10-oz.) round Gouda cheese, softened
½ cup reduced-fat sour cream
¼ cup chopped pecans
2 tablespoons milk
1 teaspoon grated onion
½ teaspoon dry mustard
Fresh parsley
Crackers or wafers

❶ With tip of sharp knife, cut scalloped pattern into wax casing of the cheese round about one-third of the way from the top. Carefully peel away upper portion of wax. Remove most of the cheese leaving a ¼-inch shell. Grate cheese on fine grater.

❷ In large bowl, beat cheese, sour cream, pecans, milk, onion and mustard at medium speed until smooth. Pour mixture into shell. Reserve extra spread as refill. Refrigerate, covered, until 30 minutes before serving. Garnish with parsley. Serve with crackers or wafers.

10 servings.

LIPTAUER CHEESE

PEGGY KREJCI
LOUDON, TENNESSEE

1 cup creamed small curd cottage cheese
½ cup soft whipped margarine
1 tablespoon chopped chives, plus more for garnish
1 teaspoon prepared mustard
1 teaspoon chopped capers
¼ teaspoon caraway seeds
⅛ teaspoon cayenne pepper
1 sweet-sour pickle, chopped
¼ teaspoon paprika
1 tablespoon grated onion
1 loaf cocktail rye bread

❶ In large bowl, beat cottage cheese and margarine at medium speed until smooth. Stir in chives, mustard, capers, caraway seeds, cayenne, pickle, paprika and onions; mix well. Refrigerate, covered, 2 hours or until thoroughly chilled. With hands, shape mixture into a ball. Garnish with additional chives. Serve with rye bread.

8 servings.

Raw &
Cooked
Veggies

BREADED MUSHROOMS WITH SHERRY

CAROL DUNNE
MIDDLE VILLAGE, NEW YORK

2 eggs
1 tablespoon sherry
1 cup dry seasoned bread crumbs
½ teaspoon garlic powder
½ teaspoon onion powder
½ cup canola oil
1 lb. white mushrooms, stems removed

❶ In small bowl, beat eggs with sherry until well blended. In another small bowl, combine bread crumbs, garlic powder and onion powder; mix well. Dip mushrooms in egg mixture, then roll in bread crumb mixture.

❷ In large skillet, heat oil over medium-high heat until hot. Add mushrooms; cook until evenly browned. Remove mushrooms to paper towel; drain. Serve with fresh parsley, if desired.

12 servings.

CHILI RELLENOS

CAROL HAWLEY
FREDERICK, MARYLAND

1 (12-oz.) can whole green chiles, drained
4 cups (1 lb.) grated Monterey Jack cheese
4 cups (1 lb.) grated cheddar cheese
4 eggs
4 tablespoons milk
2 tablespoons all-purpose flour

❶ Heat oven to 375°F. Spray 13x9-inch pan with nonstick cooking spray.

❷ Slice chiles; remove seeds and stems. Open chiles completely so they lie flat. In pan, layer chiles and cheeses, starting with light layer of cheese and ending with cheese (3 layers of cheese, 2 layers chiles).

❸ In medium bowl, beat eggs, milk and flour at medium speed until well blended. Pour egg mixture over chiles and cheese. Bake 1 hour or until firm. Cut into small squares. Serve warm.

24 servings.

CHERRY TOMATO BITES

DAVID HEPPNER
BRANDON, FLORIDA

2 pints cherry tomatoes
1 (8-oz.) pkg. cream cheese, softened
9 thick slices bacon, cooked, crumbled
¼ cup minced green onions
¼ cup minced fresh parsley
¼ teaspoon Worcestershire sauce

❶ Cut thin slice off top of each tomato. Scoop out and discard pulp. Invert tomatoes on paper towels to drain.

❷ In small bowl, combine cream cheese, bacon, onions, parsley and Worcestershire sauce; mix well. Spoon cream cheese mixture into tomatoes. Refrigerate until ready to serve.

24 servings.

POTATO ROUNDS

TINA DUKE
GLASGOW, KENTUCKY

2 to 3 large russet potatoes, cut into ¼-inch slices

Olive oil cooking spray

1 cup (4 oz.) shredded colby-Monterey Jack cheese

⅓ cup sliced green onions

¼ cup barbecue sauce

1 (8-oz.) container sour cream

6 thick slices bacon, cooked, crumbled

❶ Heat oven to 450°F. Spray both sides of potato slices with cooking spray; place on baking sheet. Bake 20 minutes or until lightly browned. Remove from oven; set aside.

❷ In large bowl, combine cheese and green onions; mix well. Using pastry brush, generously brush potatoes with barbecue sauce. Sprinkle with cheese mixture. Return potatoes to oven. Bake an additional 3 to 5 minutes or until cheese is melted. Top with sour cream; sprinkle with bacon.

12 servings.

DILLED CAULIFLOWER FLORETS

CHRIS McBEE
XENIA, OHIO

1 medium head cauliflower, broken into florets (4 cups)

¾ cup reduced-fat Italian salad dressing

1 tablespoon chopped canned pimientos

1 tablespoon finely chopped onions

½ teaspoon dried dill weed

❶ In large saucepan of boiling salted water, cook cauliflower, covered 10 minutes or until just crisp-tender; drain. Arrange florets in shallow dish.

❷ In medium bowl, combine dressing, pimientos, onions, and dill weed; mix well. Pour dressing mixture over warm cauliflower. Refrigerate, covered, several hours or overnight, stirring occasionally. Serve with toothpicks.

12 servings.

ARTICHOKE HEARTS

JUDY RICHMOND
GORHAM, MAINE

4 eggs, beaten

2 (6.5-oz.) jars marinated artichoke hearts, chopped, juice reserved

1 small onion, grated

¼ cup dry bread crumbs or cracker crumbs

½ cup (2 oz.) grated cheddar cheese

½ cup (2 oz.) freshly grated Parmesan cheese

¼ teaspoon salt

1 teaspoon hot pepper sauce

❶ Heat oven to 350°F. Spray 8-inch square pan with nonstick cooking spray.

❷ In medium bowl, combine eggs and artichoke hearts; mix well. Stir in onion, bread crumbs, cheeses, salt and hot pepper sauce; mix well. Add reserved artichoke juice; mix well. Pour mixture into pan. Bake 40 minutes or until set. Remove pan from oven; cool. Cut into 2-inch squares.

16 servings.

FRIED EGGPLANT WEDGES WITH DIJON-HORSERADISH SAUCE

FRIED EGGPLANT WEDGES WITH DIJON-HORSERADISH SAUCE

KAREN SUTCH
SALTBURG, PENNSYLVANIA

EGGPLANT
½ cup all-purpose flour
½ cup Italian-seasoned dry bread crumbs
1 teaspoon dried parsley
¼ teaspoon cayenne pepper
1 teaspoon salt
⅛ teaspoon freshly ground pepper
¼ teaspoon garlic powder
¼ teaspoon Italian seasoning, if desired
2 eggs
2 tablespoons milk
3 tablespoons extra-virgin olive oil
2 medium eggplants, peeled, sliced
¼ cup (1 oz.) freshly grated Parmesan cheese

SAUCE
¾ cup mayonnaise
¼ cup prepared horseradish
2 tablespoons Dijon mustard

❶ In large bowl, combine flour, bread crumbs, parsley, cayenne pepper, salt, ground pepper, garlic powder and Italian seasoning; mix well. In medium bowl, beat eggs and milk at medium speed until frothy.

❷ In large skillet, heat oil over medium-high heat until hot. Dip eggplant slices into egg mixture, then coat with bread mixture. Fry eggplant slices in oil about 3 minutes per side or until golden brown. (Pour additional 1 tablespoon oil in pan when turning eggplant.) Place fried eggplant on paper towels to drain and cool. Sprinkle with Parmesan cheese. Repeat until all eggplant is fried, adding oil to skillet as needed.

❸ In small bowl, combine mayonnaise, horseradish and mustard; mix well. When eggplant has cooled, cut each round into four wedges. Dip wedges in mustard mixture. Serve warm or cold.

24 servings.

CRAB-STUFFED CHERRY TOMATOES

CHRIS McBEE
XENIA, OHIO

1 pint cherry tomatoes
1 (6-oz.) can crabmeat, drained, flaked
½ green bell pepper, diced
2 green onions, sliced
2 tablespoons Italian-seasoned dry bread crumbs
1 teaspoon white wine vinegar
½ teaspoon dried parsley
¼ teaspoon dill weed
⅛ teaspoon salt

❶ Cut thin slice off tops of tomatoes; remove and discard pulp. Invert tomatoes on paper towel to drain.

❷ Heat oven to 350°F.

❸ In small bowl, combine crabmeat, bell pepper, onions, bread crumbs, vinegar, parsley, dill weed and salt; mix well. Stuff tomatoes with crabmeat mixture. Arrange tomatoes in 13x9-inch pan. Bake, uncovered, 8 to 10 minutes or until heated through and lightly browned. Serve warm.

12 servings.

CRISPY SALSA POTATO SKINS

ANNIE KIRKENDALL
KANSAS CITY, KANSAS

4 large russet potatoes
1/3 cup melted butter
1 (10-oz.) can tomatoes with green chiles, drained
1/4 cup chopped green onions
3/4 cup (3 oz.) shredded cheddar cheese
3/4 cup (3 oz.) shredded Monterey Jack cheese

❶ Pierce potatoes with fork. Microwave at High power 15 minutes, turning every 5 minutes, until potatoes are tender. Remove potatoes from microwave; cool. Cut each potato in half. Scoop out pulp, leaving 1/4-inch shell.

❷ Heat oven to 500°F. Line baking sheet with aluminum foil. Place potato shells on foil. Brush shells inside and out with butter. Bake 12 minutes or until crisp and browned.

❸ Heat broiler. In small bowl, combine tomatoes and onions; mix well. Set aside. Sprinkle potato shells with cheese. Broil 4 to 6 inches from heat 2 minutes or until cheeses are bubbly.

❹ Place potato skins on serving platter. Divide salsa evenly among potato skins. Serve immediately.

4 servings.

CRAB-STUFFED BABY PORTOBELLOS

CHARLOTTE WARD
HILTON HEAD ISLAND, SOUTH CAROLINA

24 (1-inch) baby portobello mushrooms
1 (8-oz.) pkg. cream cheese, softened
1/2 cup finely chopped green onions
1/4 cup mayonnaise
1 teaspoon fresh lemon juice
1/2 teaspoon seafood seasoning
Dash of freshly ground pepper
1 lb. canned lump crabmeat, drained, flaked
1/2 cup chopped tomatoes
1/2 cup (2 oz.) finely shredded mozzarella cheese
1/2 cup finely crushed dry stuffing mix
12 grape tomatoes, halved

❶ Heat oven to 425°F.

❷ With a spoon, remove brown gills from undersides of mushrooms; discard gills. Remove and discard stems. Set mushroom caps aside.

❸ In large bowl, beat cream cheese at medium speed until smooth. Add green onions, mayonnaise, lemon juice, seafood seasoning and pepper; mix well. Stir in crabmeat, tomatoes and cheese; mix well. Spoon mixture evenly into mushroom caps; sprinkle each cap with 1 teaspoon stuffing mix. Arrange mushrooms on baking sheet.

❹ Bake 10 minutes or until tops are lightly browned. Garnish each stuffed mushroom with halved grape tomato.

24 servings.

JALAPENO PEPPER POPPERS

MICHELLE MORRILL
PRESCOTT VALLEY, ARIZONA

1 cup (4 oz.) shredded sharp cheddar cheese
1 cup (4 oz.) shredded Monterey Jack cheese
1 (8-oz.) pkg. cream cheese, softened
4 thick slices bacon, cooked, crumbled
½ teaspoon chili powder
½ teaspoon dried oregano
3 garlic cloves, pressed
24 jalapeño chiles, halved lengthwise, seeded
½ cup dry seasoned bread crumbs
Sour cream or ranch dressing

❶ Heat oven to 300°F.

❷ In large bowl, combine shredded cheeses, cream cheese, bacon, chili powder, oregano and garlic; mix well. Spoon cheese mixture into each chile half; roll in bread crumbs. Arrange chiles, stuffed side up, on baking sheet. Bake 20 minutes for medium-spicy flavor or 40 minutes for mild flavor. Serve with sour cream or ranch dressing.

24 servings.

STUFFED CELERY

VIVIAN NIKANOW
CHICAGO, ILLINOIS

2 oz. blue cheese, softened
1 (8-oz.) pkg. cream cheese, softened
7 to 8 ribs celery, halved
Paprika

❶ In small bowl, combine cheeses. Fill celery halves with cheese mixture. Refrigerate celery several hours. Before serving, sprinkle with paprika. Cut celery into 1-inch lengths.

12 servings.

MUSHROOMS IN THE ITALIAN MANNER

GWEN CAMPBELL
STERLING, VIRGINIA

2 tablespoons olive oil
1 garlic clove, chopped
¾ lb. fresh mushrooms, thinly sliced
¼ teaspoon salt
¼ teaspoon freshly ground pepper
1 tablespoon butter
4 anchovy fillets, chopped
1 tablespoon chopped fresh Italian parsley
¼ teaspoon dried marjoram
1½ tablespoon fresh lemon juice
1 tablespoon balsamic vinegar
¼ cup freshly grated Parmesan cheese

❶ In large skillet, heat oil over medium-high heat until hot. Add garlic; lightly brown. Add mushrooms, salt and pepper; cook 4 to 5 minutes or until water from mushrooms has evaporated. Stir in butter, anchovy fillets, parsley and marjoram. Remove mixture from skillet to warmed serving platter. Sprinkle with lemon juice and balsamic vinegar. Top with Parmesan cheese.

4 servings.

PICKLED CAULIFLOWER

CHARLOTTE WARD
HILTON HEAD ISLAND, SOUTH CAROLINA

1 medium head cauliflower, cut into florets (4 cups)
1⅓ cups cider vinegar
1⅓ cups water
1 teaspoon sugar
2 garlic cloves, lightly crushed
1½ tablespoons dill seed
1½ tablespoons salt

❶ In large saucepan of boiling salted water, blanch cauliflower 1 minute; drain in colander and hold under cold running water. Place cauliflower in clean large non-reactive bowl.

❷ In medium saucepan, combine vinegar, water, sugar, garlic, dill seeds and salt. Bring to a boil over medium-high heat. Reduce heat; simmer 2 minutes.

❸ Pour vinegar mixture over cauliflower. Refrigerate, covered, at least 24 hours or up to 1 week.

10 servings.

PICKLED CARROT STICKS

CHARLOTTE WARD
HILTON HEAD ISLAND, SOUTH CAROLINA

1 lb. carrots, cut into 3½-x⅓-inch sticks
1 cup cider vinegar
1¼ cups water
¼ cup sugar
2 garlic cloves, lightly crushed
1½ tablespoons dill seeds
2 teaspoons salt

❶ In large saucepan of boiling salted water, blanch carrots 1 minute; drain in colander and hold under cold running water.

❷ In large saucepan, combine vinegar, 1¼ cups water, sugar, garlic, dill seeds and salt; bring to a boil over medium-high heat. Reduce heat to medium; simmer 2 minutes.

❸ Pour vinegar mixture over carrots. Refrigerate, covered, at least 24 hours or up to 1 week.

10 servings.

MARINATED ARTICHOKE HEARTS

CHARLOTTE WARD
HILTON HEAD ISLAND, SOUTH CAROLINA

¼ cup olive oil
¼ cup white wine vinegar
⅛ teaspoon salt
⅛ teaspoon freshly ground pepper
¼ teaspoon dried parsley
⅛ teaspoon dried whole oregano
⅛ teaspoon dried whole basil
⅛ teaspoon dried whole marjoram
1 (14-oz.) can artichoke hearts, drained, quartered

❶ In jar, combine oil, vinegar, salt, pepper, parsley, oregano, basil and marjoram. Cover tightly; shake vigorously.

❷ In 13x9-inch pan, arrange artichokes in single layer; drizzle marinade over artichokes. Refrigerate, covered, 8 hours. Drain and discard marinade before serving.

6 servings.

PICKLED CAULIFLOWER, PICKLED CARROT STICKS & MARINATED ARTICHOKE HEARTS

BREADED ARTICHOKE HEARTS

ROSE DEVITO
LONG BRANCH, NEW JERSEY

2 eggs

1 tablespoon freshly grated Parmesan cheese

2 (9-oz.) pkg. frozen artichoke hearts, thawed, drained

2 cups dry seasoned bread crumbs

3 to 4 tablespoons olive oil

❶ Heat oven to 350°F. Spray 13x9-inch pan with nonstick cooking spray.

❷ In medium bowl, beat eggs and cheese at medium speed until well blended. Dip artichoke hearts in egg mixture, then roll in bread crumbs. Arrange artichoke hearts in pan; drizzle with oil. Bake 15 to 20 minutes or until golden brown.

10 servings.

BAKED POTATO SKINS

CHRIS McBEE
XENIA, OHIO

8 russet potatoes

1/2 cup butter, melted

1/2 teaspoon salt

1/2 teaspoon paprika

1/2 cup finely chopped green onions

1/2 cup cooked crumbled bacon

1/2 cup chopped ham

1/2 cup chopped green bell peppers

1 cup (4 oz.) shredded cheddar cheese

1 (8-oz.) container sour cream

❶ Heat oven to 400°F.

❷ Bake potatoes 1 hour or until tender. Cool slightly; cut in half lengthwise. Scoop out pulp, leaving 1/4-inch shell. Cut skins into strips or halves; brush skin sides with melted butter. Place skins on baking sheet. Sprinkle pulp sides with salt, paprika, green onions, bacon, ham, bell peppers and cheese. Increase oven temperature to 450°F. Bake 10 to 15 minutes or until cheese is melted and skins are crisp. Top each with dollop of sour cream.

6 to 10 servings.

FRENCH FRIED CAULIFLOWER APPETIZERS

AUDREY DERR
VALRICO, FLORIDA

1 egg, beaten

2 cups milk

1 medium head cauliflower, cut into florets (4 cups)

2 cups all-purpose flour

Vegetable oil for frying

1/8 teaspoon salt

Cocktail sauce

❶ In large bowl, beat egg and milk at medium speed until well blended. Add cauliflower to egg mixture; mix well. Refrigerate, covered, 2 hours.

❷ Remove cauliflower from egg mixture. Place about half of the florets in large resealable plastic bag. Add half of the flour; seal bag. Shake until cauliflower is well coated. Remove cauliflower from bag; arrange in single layer on baking sheet. Repeat with remaining florets and flour. Freeze florets, covered, on baking sheet 2 hours or until solidly frozen.

❸ In deep skillet or deep fryer, heat 2 inches of oil until hot. Cook cauliflower in oil until browned. Drain on paper towels. Sprinkle with salt. Serve with cocktail sauce.

12 servings.

CRAB-STUFFED MUSHROOMS

LISA ALDERFER
FORT WORTH, TEXAS

16 large mushroom caps
⅓ cup butter, melted
½ lb. canned lump crabmeat, drained, flaked
2 eggs
3 tablespoons mayonnaise
⅓ cup chives
2 teaspoons fresh lemon juice
½ cup dry bread crumbs

❶ Heat oven to 375°F. Spray 13x9-inch pan with nonstick cooking spray.

❷ Dip mushrooms in melted butter. Arrange mushrooms, cap side up, on pan. In medium bowl, combine crabmeat, eggs, mayonnaise, chives, lemon juice and bread crumbs; mix well. Fill mushroom caps with crabmeat mixture. Drizzle remaining butter over tops of mushrooms. Bake, uncovered, 15 minutes. Serve hot.

16 servings.

STUFFED ARTICHOKES

ANNIE KIRKENDALL
KANSAS CITY, KANSAS

1 cup dry bread crumbs
4 tablespoons grated Romano cheese
2 garlic cloves, crushed
2 tablespoons chopped fresh parsley
4 artichokes, tips and chokes removed, stems trimmed
6 tablespoons olive oil

❶ In large bowl, combine bread crumbs, cheese, garlic and parsley; mix well. Stuff artichoke leaves with bread crumb mixture. Place stuffed leaves in large pot. Fill pot with water 1½ inches below top of artichokes. Dribble 1 tablespoon of the oil over artichokes. Pour remaining 5 tablespoons oil into water. Boil 30 to 45 minutes over medium-high heat or until bottom leaves fall off when pierced with fork.

4 servings.

MUSHROOMS PARMESAN

LORRAINE MAGUR
WASHINGTONVILLE, NEW YORK

1 lb. mushrooms, stems removed, finely chopped
4 tablespoons olive oil
¼ cup chopped onions
½ garlic clove, minced
⅓ cup dry bread crumbs
3 tablespoons freshly grated Parmesan cheese
1 tablespoon chopped fresh parsley
½ teaspoon salt
⅛ teaspoon oregano

❶ Heat oven to 400°F. Spray 1½-quart casserole with nonstick cooking spray.

❷ Place mushroom caps, open side up, in casserole; set aside.

❸ In large skillet, heat 2 tablespoons of the oil over medium-high heat until hot. Add mushroom stems, onions and garlic; sauté until onions are tender.

❹ In medium bowl, combine bread crumbs, cheese, parsley, salt and oregano; mix well. Stir in mushroom mixture. Spoon mixture evenly into mushroom caps. Pour remaining 2 tablespoons oil in casserole. Bake 15 to 20 minutes or until mushrooms are tender and tops are browned.

6 to 8 servings.

CORN AND RED ONION FRITTERS WITH PIMIENTO-JALAPENO SAUCE

CORN AND RED ONION FRITTERS WITH PIMIENTO-JALAPENO SAUCE

CAROLYN LYONS
BROCKTON, MASSACHUSETTS

FRITTERS

3 cups all-purpose flour

1 cup cake flour

2 tablespoons baking powder

1 teaspoon salt

2 eggs

2 cups diced red onions

3 cups fresh corn kernels or canned corn, juice reserved

1½ cups milk

1½ quarts soy oil

SAUCE

4 tablespoons unsalted butter

3 tablespoons all-purpose flour

2 cups milk

½ cup (2 oz.) grated sharp cheddar cheese

1 (4-oz.) jar chopped pimientos

½ cup chopped pickled jalapeño chiles, juice reserved

❶ In large bowl, sift together 2 cups all-purpose flour, 1 cup cake flour, baking powder and salt. Stir in eggs, onions and corn; mix well. Moisten with just enough milk to produce a sticky batter.

❷ In medium saucepan or deep fryer, heat oil to 375°F. Carefully drop fritters by generous teaspoonful into hot oil. Fry 5 minutes or until golden brown.

❸ In 2-quart saucepan, melt butter over medium-low heat. Stir in ¼ cup flour; cook 10 minutes, stirring constantly, taking care that flour does not brown. Meanwhile, heat 2 cups milk to just under a boil; remove from heat.

❹ Add milk to flour mixture, whisking constantly, until sauce is completely smooth. Add cheese; stir until melted. Stir in pimientos and chiles. Serve with fritters.

12 servings.

MARINATED BROCCOLI

CHARLOTTE WARD
HILTON HEAD ISLAND, SOUTH CAROLINA

1 cup cider vinegar

1 tablespoon sugar

1 tablespoon whole dried dill weed

1 teaspoon salt

1 teaspoon garlic salt

1 teaspoon freshly ground pepper

1½ cups vegetable oil

½ lb. broccoli florets

❶ In medium bowl, combine vinegar, sugar, dill weed, salt, garlic salt, pepper and oil; mix well. Pour mixture over broccoli; toss gently to evenly coat. Refrigerate, covered, at least 24 hours, stirring several times.

10 to 12 servings.

VEGGIE FRITTERS

SHAMSA PIRANI
ATLANTA, GEORGIA

¾ cup all-purpose flour

⅔ cup milk

1 egg

1 tablespoon vegetable oil, plus more for frying

¼ teaspoon salt

3 cups sliced cooked potatoes (¼ inch thick)

3 cups sliced cooked eggplant (¼ inch thick)

3 cups sliced cooked zucchini (¼ inch thick)

Vegetable oil for frying

❶ In medium bowl, combine flour, milk, egg, 1 tablespoon oil and salt; beat at medium speed until just smooth.

❷ In large skillet heat 1½ inches oil to 365°F. Dip vegetable slices in flour mixture, shaking off excess. Fry vegetables, a few slices at a time, in single layer 3 to 4 minutes or until golden. Remove vegetables from oil; drain on paper towels.

12 servings.

VEGGIE BARS

CAROL HAWLEY
FREDERICK, MARYLAND

1 (8-oz.) can refrigerated crescent roll dough

1 (8-oz.) pkg. plus 1 (3-oz.) pkg. cream cheese, softened

1/2 cup mayonnaise

1 (1-oz.) pkg. ranch dressing mix

3/4 cup chopped green onions

3/4 cup chopped plum tomatoes

3/4 cups chopped cauliflower

3/4 cup chopped broccoli

3/4 cup (3 oz.) shredded cheddar cheese

❶ Spray 13x9-inch pan with nonstick cooking spray. Press dough into bottom of pan. Bake according to package directions.

❷ In medium bowl, combine cream cheese, mayonnaise and dressing mix; mix well. Spread mixture over cooled crust. Press vegetables into cream cheese. Cut into squares. Top with cheddar cheese.

24 servings.

SPINACH-STUFFED MUSHROOMS

DAVID HEPPNER
BRANDON, FLORIDA

1 tablespoon margarine

14 large mushrooms, stems removed, chopped

1 garlic clove, minced

1 teaspoon Worcestershire sauce

1/2 cup dry bread crumbs

1 teaspoon prepared mustard

1/8 teaspoon freshly ground pepper

2 tablespoons reduced-fat mayonnaise

2 tablespoons freshly grated Parmesan cheese

1 (10-oz.) pkg. frozen chopped spinach, thawed, drained

❶ Heat oven to 350°F.

❷ In medium skillet, melt margarine over medium heat. Add mushrooms, mushroom stems and garlic; sauté until tender. Remove mushroom mixture from skillet; set aside. Add Worcestershire sauce, bread crumbs, mustard, pepper, mayonnaise and cheese to skillet. Stir in spinach. Spoon mixture into each cap. Arrange mushrooms in 11x7-inch baking pan. Pour 3/4 cup water in bottom of pan. Bake, uncovered, 20 minutes or until mushrooms are hot. Remove from pan; discard liquid.

7 servings.

SPINACH BALLS

NANCY HROMADA
AFTON, NEW YORK

2 (10-oz.) pkg. frozen chopped spinach, thawed, drained

2 3/4 to 3 cups dry stuffing mix

6 eggs, beaten

1 cup butter, melted

1 medium onion, finely grated

1 garlic clove, minced

1/2 cup (2 oz.) grated Romano cheese

1/2 cup (2 oz.) freshly grated Parmesan cheese

❶ Heat oven to 350°F. Line baking sheet with aluminum foil; spray with nonstick cooking spray.

❷ In large bowl, combine spinach, stuffing mix, eggs, butter, onion, garlic and cheeses; mix well. With hands, form mixture into 1-inch balls. Arrange on baking sheet. Bake 25 to 30 minutes or until set, lightly browned and cheese is melted.

16 servings.

ONIONS STUFFED WITH MUSHROOMS

DAVID HEPPNER
BRANDON, FLORIDA

1/4 cup water

12 small onions, peeled

1 1/2 cups mushrooms, finely chopped

2 garlic cloves, minced

4 tablespoons dry bread crumbs

3 tablespoons freshly grated Parmesan cheese

2 tablespoons chopped fresh parsley

2 tablespoons chopped fresh oregano

1 teaspoon spike seasoning or your favorite seasoned salt

1/2 teaspoon freshly ground pepper

❶ Heat oven to 350°F. Spray 13x9-inch pan with nonstick cooking spray.

❷ In medium saucepan, pour water over onions; bring to simmer over medium-high heat. Steam onions 20 to 30 minutes or until fork-tender; drain and cool.

❸ In small bowl, combine mushrooms, garlic, bread crumbs, cheese, parsley, oregano, spike seasoning and pepper; mix well.

❹ Cut onions in half crosswise. Scoop pulp, leaving shell of 3 to 4 layers and bottom intact. Finely chop 1/2 cup of pulp; discard remaining pulp. Add 1/2 cup pulp to mushroom mixture. Spoon mixture evenly into onions. Arrange onions on pan. Bake, uncovered, 20 minutes. Serve warm.

6 servings.

MARINATED MUSHROOMS

LAWRENCE ASHBAUGH
TULSA, OKLAHOMA

3/4 cup olive oil

1/3 cup wine vinegar

2 garlic cloves, crushed

1 bay leaf

3/4 teaspoon sugar

1/2 teaspoon salt

1/2 teaspoon dried basil

1 teaspoon chili powder

6 whole peppercorns

1 1/2 lb. medium mushrooms

❶ In Dutch oven, combine oil, vinegar, garlic, bay leaf, sugar, salt, basil, chili powder and peppercorns; bring to a boil over medium-high heat. Reduce heat; simmer 10 minutes. Stir in mushrooms; simmer 5 minutes. Refrigerate, covered, overnight. Remove and discard bay leaf before serving.

12 servings.

CUCUMBER APPETIZER

SHEILA SLOAN
HULL, GEORGIA

1/2 teaspoon salt

3 medium cucumbers, halved lengthwise, seeded, sliced

5 green onions, finely chopped

Dash of freshly ground pepper

1/4 teaspoon ground cumin

1/4 teaspoon chili powder

1/4 teaspoon ground cloves

1 cup plain yogurt

❶ Lightly salt cucumbers; let stand 20 minutes. Thoroughly squeeze excess moisture from cucumbers.

❷ In medium bowl, combine green onions, pepper, cumin, chili powder, cloves and yogurt; blend well. Refrigerate sauce and cucumbers separately. Serve cucumbers in individual dishes topped with yogurt sauce.

6 servings.

BRIE-STUFFED MUSHROOMS

MILLIE BROOKS
NORRIS CITY, ILLINOIS

8 tablespoons butter

½ cup chopped walnuts

3 garlic cloves, minced

¼ cup minced fresh parsley

¼ cup minced green onions

⅛ teaspoon salt

⅛ teaspoon ground white pepper

16 medium or large mushroom caps

8 oz. Brie cheese, cut into ½-inch pieces

❶ Heat oven to 350°F.

❷ In large skillet, melt 2 tablespoons of the butter over medium heat. Add walnuts; sauté 3 to 5 minutes or until toasted. Set aside.

❸ In another large skillet, melt remaining 6 tablespoons butter over medium-high heat. Add garlic, parsley, green onions, salt and pepper; sauté until onions are tender. Stir in mushrooms; briefly sauté, coating well with butter. Remove mushroom mixture to ovenproof serving platter. Sprinkle cheese over mushrooms. Bake 10 minutes or until cheese melts. Sprinkle with walnuts.

8 servings.

VEGETABLE CHEESECAKE BARS

RAQUEL PRYSZCZUK
PALO ALTO, CALIFORNIA

1½ cups all-purpose flour

1 teaspoon salt

1 teaspoon baking powder

½ cup butter

2 tablespoons vegetable shortening

1 egg

3 tablespoons olive oil

1 cup minced onions

1 cup grated carrots

3 medium zucchini, grated

½ teaspoon freshly ground pepper

¼ cup green onions

5 garlic cloves, minced

3 (8-oz.) pkg. cream cheese

4 cups (16 oz.) ricotta cheese

1 cup (4 oz.) feta cheese

4 eggs

4 plum tomatoes, peeled, sliced into rounds

4 to 6 tablespoons dry bread crumbs

4 tablespoons fresh chopped parsley

❶ Heat oven to 350°F.

❷ In food processor, combine flour, salt and baking powder. Add butter and shortening; pulse until mixture crumbles. Add egg; mix until dough forms a ball. Press dough into 13x9-inch pan. Bake 10 minutes. Remove crust from oven. Reduce oven temperature to 325°F.

❸ In large skillet, heat oil over medium-high heat until hot. Add onions; sauté until tender. Add carrots, zucchini and pepper; cook an additional 3 to 4 minutes or until vegetables are tender. Add green onions and garlic; cook an additional 2 minutes.

❹ Meanwhile, wash food processor bowl. Combine cream cheese, ricotta, feta and eggs in food processor; process until smooth. Pour cream cheese mixture into large bowl. In same food processor, add onion mixture; process until smooth; mix well. Remove dough-lined pan from refrigerator; pour filling into pan. Arrange tomato slices on filling; sprinkle with bread crumbs. Bake 1 hour or until center is firm. Serve warm or at room temperature. Garnish with parsley.

48 servings.

VEGETABLE CHEESECAKE BARS

ZUCCHINI SQUARES APPETIZER

CAROL HAWLEY
FREDERICK, MARYLAND

2$\frac{1}{2}$ cups grated unpeeled zucchini

$\frac{1}{2}$ cup chopped onions

1 garlic clove, minced

$\frac{1}{3}$ cup butter, melted

3 eggs, slightly beaten

1 teaspoon chopped fresh basil or $\frac{1}{2}$ teaspoon dried

$\frac{1}{2}$ teaspoon cayenne pepper

$\frac{1}{2}$ teaspoon salt

1 cup all-purpose flour

$\frac{1}{2}$ teaspoon baking powder

1 cup (4 oz.) grated cheddar, Monterey Jack or Muenster cheese

$\frac{1}{4}$ cup (1 oz.) freshly grated Parmesan cheese

❶ In large bowl, combine zucchini, onion, garlic, butter and eggs; mix well. In small bowl, stir together basil, cayenne, salt, flour and baking powder. Stir basil mixture into zucchini mixture; mix well. Stir in cheese; mix well.

❷ Pour mixture into 13x9-inch microwave-safe pan. Sprinkle with Parmesan cheese. Cover pan with parchment paper; microwave at High power 7 to 10 minutes, rotating halfway through cooking time, or until mixture is set, vegetables are tender and cheese is melted. Cool 10 minutes before cutting into squares.

36 servings.

QUICHE-STUFFED MUSHROOMS

VICKI WILLIAMSON
BELLINGHAM, WASHINGTON

2 lb. large mushrooms, stems removed, chopped

6 tablespoons butter, melted

2 tablespoons finely minced onion

2 eggs, slightly beaten

$\frac{1}{2}$ cup whipping cream

$\frac{1}{4}$ teaspoon salt

$\frac{1}{4}$ teaspoon freshly ground pepper

4 thick slices bacon, cooked, crumbled

$\frac{1}{2}$ cup (2 oz.) shredded Swiss cheese

❶ Heat oven to 350°F.

❷ Dry mushroom caps thoroughly with paper towels; brush with butter. Arrange caps in 13x9-inch pan, hollow side up. Heat remaining butter in large skillet over medium-high heat. Add onion and mushroom stems; sauté 3 to 5 minutes or until onions are tender.

❸ In medium bowl, combine eggs, whipping cream, salt and pepper; beat well. Stir in bacon, onion and mushroom-stem mixture. Stir in Swiss cheese. Spoon mixture carefully into prepared mushroom caps. Bake 30 minutes or until filling is set.

12 servings.

Wraps,
Rolls
& Folds

ARMADILLO EGGS

PATTE MARTIN
DONNA, TEXAS

18 small pickled jalapeño chiles, seeded, stems removed
4 cups (1 lb.) shredded cheddar cheese
1 cup baking mix
1 lb. bulk pork sausage

❶ Heat oven to 450°F. Spray baking sheet with non-stick cooking spray.

❷ In large bowl, combine chiles and half of the cheese; mix well. In another large bowl, combine baking mix, sausage and remainder of the cheese; mix well.

❸ With hands, form mixture into small, thin patties. Enclose 1 chile and cheese completely into each patty. Place patties on baking sheet. Bake, uncovered, 10 minutes or until patties start to brown; turn and pour off grease. Cook an additional 10 to 15 minutes or until sausage is no longer pink in center. Serve hot.

18 servings.

PICKLE ROLLS

CRYSTAL FITZHUGH
BRENTWOOD, CALIFORNIA

2 (2.5-oz.) pkg. thin dry beef
1 (8-oz.) pkg. cream cheese, softened
10 to 15 baby kosher dills

❶ Unfold beef and separate slices. Spread cream cheese evenly over each slice. Place dills on edge of slice; roll up. Slice rolls-ups into ¼-inch pieces.

12 servings.

SHRIMP AND AVOCADO QUESADILLAS

DIANE FELKER
NEW HYDE PARK, NEW YORK

4 cups (1 lb.) shredded cheddar cheese
8 burrito-size flour tortillas
1 large ripe avocado, sliced
1 lb. shelled, deveined cooked medium shrimp
2 ripe tomatoes, chopped
6 green onions, minced
Sour cream

❶ Heat oven to 350°F.

❷ Sprinkle ¼ cup cheese evenly onto 4 of the tortillas. Divide and arrange 2 slices avocado, 4 to 5 pieces shrimp, chopped tomatoes and green onions in single layer among the tortillas. Sprinkle with an additional ¼ cup cheese on each; top each with another tortilla.

❸ Place tortillas on baking sheet. Bake, uncovered, 10 to 15 minutes, or until cheese is melted. Remove tortillas from oven; cut into wedges. Serve with sour cream.

24 servings.

STEPH-TIAS (SOUTHWESTERN TOSTADAS)

STEPHANIE ALLEE
HAGERSTOWN, MARYLAND

1½ cups diced cooked chicken

1 (15-oz.) can black beans, drained, rinsed

1 (10-oz.) pkg. frozen chopped spinach, thawed, drained

1⅓ cups frozen corn, thawed

2 tablespoons chopped green chiles

½ teaspoons garlic powder

2 cups (8 oz.) finely shredded cheddar-Monterey Jack cheese

10 (8-inch) flour tortillas

Sour cream

❶ Heat oven to 400°F.

❷ In large bowl, combine chicken, beans, spinach, corn, chiles, garlic powder and about ⅓ cup of the cheese with fork; mix well.

❸ Spray both sides of tortilla with cooking spray; place on baking sheet. Bake, uncovered, 5 minutes or until very lightly browned. Remove tortillas from oven; flip over but do not return to oven. Repeat with remaining tortillas.

❹ Spread about ¼ cup of the bean mixture evenly over tops of each tortilla. Sprinkle with cheese. Return tortillas to oven; cook, uncovered, 5 to 8 minutes or until cheese is melted. Cut with knife or pizza wheel into quarters. Serve with sour cream.

20 servings.

SCALLION-STUFFED BEEF ROLLS

DIANE FELKER
NEW HYDE PARK, NEW YORK

½ cup sugar

½ cup low-sodium soy sauce

½ cup rice vinegar

1 tablespoon finely minced fresh ginger

1 lb. partially frozen London broil beef (or beef top round, cut on angle)

12 scallions, trimmed, cut into 1½-inch lengths

❶ Heat broiler. Lightly oil broiler pan. In medium saucepan, dissolve sugar in soy sauce and vinegar over medium heat. Add ginger; increase heat to medium high. Boil 5 to 8 minutes until mixture is reduced to ¾ cup. Set aside.

❷ Using sharp knife, cut beef into paper-thin strips 5x1½ inches. Place 1 scallion piece at one end of each strip; roll up tightly. Arrange rolls, seam-side down, on pan. Pour soy sauce mixture over roll-ups.

❸ Broil 4 to 6 inches from heat 4 to 5 minutes, turning once, until beef is brown. Insert toothpick into each roll-up. Serve warm.

10 servings.

POCKET QUESADILLAS

KIMBERLEY GALLAGHER
MOUNTLAKE TERRACE, WASHINGTON

1 tablespoon olive oil

½ teaspoon chili powder

4 boneless skinless chicken breast halves

1 (16-oz.) can fat-free refried beans

½ teaspoon cayenne pepper

4 pita breads, split

2 cups (8 oz.) grated Monterey Jack cheese

¼ cup chopped ripe olives, if desired

¼ cup chopped jalapeno chiles, if desired

❶ Heat grill. In small bowl, combine oil and chili powder; mix well. Brush oil mixture evenly over chicken. Place chicken on gas grill over medium heat or on charcoal grill 4 to 6 inches from medium coals. Cook 8 to 10 minutes or until chicken juices run clear, turning once. Remove chicken from grill. Cut into 1-inch pieces. Set aside.

❷ In medium saucepan, heat beans and cayenne over medium heat, stirring frequently, until hot.

❸ Heat broiler. Spoon 2 tablespoons beans evenly into each pita. Stuff with chicken, cheese, olives and chiles. Arrange pitas on baking sheet. Broil 4 to 6 inches from heat 2 to 3 minutes or until crisps, turning once. Serve hot or cold.

8 servings.

MEXICAN EGG ROLLS

ORPHA WORLF
BRAINARD, NEBRASKA

2 lb. ground beef

1 medium onion, finely chopped

2 (1.25-oz.) pkg. taco seasoning mix

1½ cups water

1 (16-oz.) can refried beans

2 (1-lb.) pkg. egg roll wrappers

Vegetable oil for frying

❶ In large skillet, cook ground beef and onions over medium-high heat until beef is no longer pink. Remove mixture from skillet; drain. Return mixture to skillet. Add taco seasoning and water; simmer 3 minutes or until mixture has thickened. Remove from heat. Add refried beans; cool.

❷ Separate egg roll wrappers. Spread 2 tablespoons beef mixture evenly into each wrapper. Fold in ends; roll up.

❸ In large skillet or deep fryer, heat oil to 370°F. Add egg rolls; fry 8 to 10 minutes or until crispy, brown and bubbly. Serve warm with sour cream.

24 servings.

CHICKEN MINI SHELLS

JUDY RICHMOND
GORHAM, MAINE

1 (5-oz.) can shredded cooked chicken

1 tablespoon mayonnaise

1 teaspoon dill

½ teaspoon garlic powder

¼ teaspoon salt

¼ teaspoon freshly ground pepper

½ cup crushed walnuts

1 tablespoon sugar

8 frozen miniature phyllo dough shells, thawed

❶ In large bowl, combine chicken, mayonnaise, dill, garlic, salt, pepper, walnuts and sugar; mix well.

❷ Refrigerate, covered, 1 hour or until chilled.

❸ Fill shells evenly with chicken mixture just before serving. Garnish with greens.

4 servings.

SHRIMP EGG ROLLS

KAY SNYDER
BEMIDJI, MINNESOTA

1 tablespoon oil

2 lb. shelled, deveined uncooked medium shrimp, finely chopped

6 to 8 green tomatoes, finely chopped

1 cup chopped bean sprouts

$1/2$ cup finely chopped water chestnuts

$1^{1}/2$ tablespoons low-sodium soy sauce

2 (1-lb.) pkg. egg roll wrappers

Vegetable oil

Sour cream

❶ In large skillet, heat oil over medium-high heat until hot. Add shrimp and tomatoes; fry about 3 minutes or until shrimp turn pink.

❷ Stir in bean sprouts, water chestnuts and soy sauce. Spread 1 tablespoon shrimp filling evenly along edge of each wrapper. Fold in ends; roll tightly. Use a little water to seal wrapper.

❸ Heat oil in wok or deep fryer to 370°F. Add egg rolls; fry 8 to 10 minutes or until crispy, brown and bubbly.

24 servings.

TARRAGON CLAM ROLLS

NANCY TYBOROWSKI
WAKEFIELD, RHODE ISLAND

1 tablespoon butter

$1^{1}/2$ tablespoons chopped shallots

1 tablespoon fresh tarragon or $1/2$ teaspoon dried

2 tablespoons all-purpose flour

1 teaspoon Worcestershire sauce

Dash of mace

1 (8-oz.) can minced clams, undrained

14 slices white bread, crusts removed

$1/4$ cup butter, melted

1 teaspoon paprika

❶ Heat oven to 425°F.

❷ In large skillet, melt butter over medium-high heat. Add shallots and tarragon; sauté until shallots are tender. Stir in flour, Worcestershire sauce and mace; mix well. Add clams and liquid. Cook over medium heat until mixture thickens, stirring occasionally. Remove skillet from heat; cool.

❸ Flatten bread with rolling pin until thin. Brush with butter and 1 tablespoon of the shallot mixture. Roll tightly, cut into 3 sections. Brush with melted butter, sprinkle with paprika. Place roll-ups on baking sheet. Bake, uncovered, 10 minutes. Serve warm.

14 servings.

CHEESY CHILI CUPS

JACKIE CHEEK
PAOLA, KANSAS

24 wonton wrappers, cut into 3½-inch rounds
1 cup (4 oz.) shredded cheddar cheese
⅓ cup ricotta cheese
¼ cup green chiles, drained, chopped
1 tablespoon chives or green onion tops, chopped
¼ teaspoon ground cumin
48 ripe olives, sliced

❶ Heat oven to 350°F. Spray 24 (1¾-inch) miniature muffin cups with nonstick cooking spray. Press each wonton into bottom and up sides of each muffin cup. Bake, uncovered, 7 to 8 minutes or until lightly browned. Remove wontons from cups; cool on baking sheet.

❷ In medium bowl, combine cheeses, chiles, chives and cumin; mix well. Fill each wonton evenly with 2 teaspoons of the cheese filling. Top with 2 olive slices. Bake an additional 10 minutes. Serve warm.

12 servings.

ROAST BEEF 'N SWISS TORTILLA ROLL-UPS

JESSICA BRANDER
ZEELAND, NORTH DAKOTA

2 tablespoons Caesar ranch salad dressing
2 (8-inch) flour tortilla
2 large leaf lettuce leaves, torn to fit tortilla
4 oz. thinly sliced deli roast beef
4 slices pasteurized process Swiss cheese
2 teaspoons diced red onion

❶ Spread 1 tablespoon salad dressing evenly over each tortilla, covering entire surface. Top each with lettuce, slice of roast beef, cheese and onion. Roll up each tortilla tightly; secure with toothpick. To serve, cut into 1-inch slices.

8 servings.

LUMPIA

JEAN McCLEAN
WOODSIDE, NEW YORK

½ lb. bulk sweet Italian sausage
½ lb. hot bulk Italian sausage
4 green onions, chopped
1 tablespoon low-sodium soy sauce
2 teaspoons adobo seasoning
⅛ teaspoon salt
⅛ teaspoon freshly ground pepper
25 spring roll wrappers, thawed
Vegetable oil for frying
Duck sauce

❶ In large skillet, cook sausage over medium-high heat until slightly pink. Add green onions; cook, stirring occasionally, until onions are tender and sausage is no longer pink. Season with soy sauce, adobo seasoning, salt and pepper.

❷ Spread about 1 tablespoon sausage mixture evenly into each wrapper; roll according to package directions. Seal with water.

❸ In another large skillet, heat oil over medium-high heat until hot. Add wontons; fry until golden brown. Serve with duck sauce.

12 servings.

CRISPY WONTONS WITH ORIENTAL PEACH SAUCE

CRISPY WONTONS WITH ORIENTAL PEACH SAUCE

YEN YEN NG
MESA, ARIZONA

FILLING
3/4 lb. ground pork
1 tablespoon oyster sauce
1 teaspoon low-sodium soy sauce
1 teaspoon sugar
1/2 teaspoon salt
1/4 teaspoon freshly ground pepper
1 1/2 tablespoons cornstarch
1 large garlic clove, minced
1/2 teaspoon grated fresh ginger
1 teaspoon toasted sesame oil
1 (5-oz.) can water chestnuts, finely chopped
1/2 cup finely chopped green onions

SAUCE
1 (15-oz.) can sliced peaches, drained
3 tablespoons teriyaki sauce
1 tablespoon cornstarch
1 tablespoon sugar
1/4 teaspoon five-spice powder
1/4 teaspoon freshly ground pepper

WONTONS
2 (1-lb.) pkg. wonton wrappers
Vegetable oil for frying

❶ In large bowl, combine pork, oyster sauce, soy sauce, 1 teaspoon sugar, salt, 1/4 teaspoon pepper, 1 1/2 tablespoons cornstarch, garlic, ginger, oil, water chestnuts and onions; mix well. In large skillet, sauté filling mixture over medium heat 3 to 4 minutes or until pork is no longer pink in center. Remove skillet from heat; cool slightly.

❷ To make sauce, place peaches, teriyaki sauce, 1 tablespoon cornstarch, 1 tablespoon sugar, five-spice powder, and 1/4 teaspoon pepper in blender. Cover and blend on high speed until smooth. Pour peach mixture into small saucepan; bring to a boil over medium heat. Simmer about 2 minutes, stirring constantly, until sauce thickens. Remove from heat.

❸ Spread 1 tablespoon filling mixture evenly into center of each wrapper. Wet edges; fold wrapper over filling to form a triangle and seal edges. Wet the 2 folded corners and draw the ends together to make a bow-like dumpling similar to a tortellini.

❹ Heat oil in large skillet or deep fryer to 375°F. Add wontons; fry wontons, a few at a time, 2 to 3 minutes or until golden brown and crispy outside and pork is no longer pink inside. Drain on paper towels. Serve with warm sauce.

20 servings.

DEEP-FRIED SAMOSAS

SUSAN ARNETT
CIRCLE PINES, MINNESOTA

1 teaspoon all-purpose flour
2 tablespoons water
1 lb. ground beef, cooked, drained
1 medium onion, finely chopped
1 garlic clove, finely chopped
1 teaspoon salt
1/2 teaspoon ground coriander
1/4 teaspoon ground cumin
1/4 teaspoon ground ginger
1/4 teaspoon freshly ground pepper
1 (1-lb.) pkg. wonton wrappers
Vegetable oil for frying
Chutney or sweet and sour sauce for dipping

❶ In small bowl, whisk together flour and water to make a thin paste.

❷ In large bowl, combine beef, onion, garlic, salt, coriander, cumin, ginger and pepper; mix well. Spread 1 teaspoon meat mixture evenly into center of each wrapper. Using flour paste, seal edges of wrapper to form triangle. Fold 2 side points into the middle; paste down.

❸ In wok or large skillet, heat oil to 375°F. Add wontons; fry until light golden. Serve with chutney or sweet and sour sauce.

10 servings.

BAKED POT STICKERS AND DIPPING SAUCE

MICHELLE MORRILL
PRESCOTT VALLEY, ARIZONA

1 tablespoon finely grated carrot
1/2 lb. sliced turkey, diced
2 garlic cloves, minced
2 teaspoons minced fresh ginger
3 tablespoons sour cream
2 egg whites
1/4 cup sliced green onions
1 tablespoon low-sodium soy sauce
24 wonton wrappers

DIPPING SAUCE
1 teaspoon minced fresh ginger
3/4 cup sour cream
3 tablespoons low-sodium soy sauce
1 tablespoon white wine vinegar
2 teaspoons sliced green onions
1 1/2 teaspoons sugar

❶ Heat oven to 400°F. Lightly spray baking sheet with nonstick cooking spray.

❷ In medium bowl, combine carrot, turkey, garlic, 2 teaspoons ginger, 3 tablespoons sour cream, 1 of the egg whites, 1/4 cup green onions and 1 tablespoon soy sauce; mix well. Place 1 wonton wrapper on cutting board. Lightly brush with beaten egg white. Spread 1 teaspoon carrot mixture evenly into each wrapper; fold over, pressing to seal triangle. Arrange 2 filled wontons back to back. Using round cutter, cut off top edges. Continue with remaining wontons and filling.

❸ Place wontons on baking sheet. Bake, uncovered, 20 minutes or until lightly browned.

❹ In medium bowl, combine ginger, sour cream, soy sauce, vinegar, onions and sugar; mix well. Serve with ginger mixture.

12 servings.

CHICKEN CAESAR TORTILLAS

REBECCA JACOBS
FORT RUCKER, ALABAMA

2 garlic cloves, minced

1 teaspoon freshly ground pepper

3 boneless skinless chicken breast halves

¼ cup sliced ripe olives

½ medium red onion, sliced thinly

¼ cup freshly grated Parmesan cheese

4 cups romaine lettuce, thinly sliced

½ cup Caesar salad dressing

6 (8-inch) flour tortillas

24 whole medium ripe olives

❶ Heat grill. In small bowl, combine garlic and pepper; mix well. Press mixture into chicken. Place chicken on gas grill over medium-high heat or on charcoal grill 4 to 6 inches from medium coals. Cook chicken 7 to 8 minutes, turning once, or until juices run clear. Cool and slice chicken.

❷ In large bowl, combine sliced olives, onion, cheese and lettuce; mix well. Add dressing; toss until well coated. Divide salad equally over tortillas. Roll tortillas up tightly, jelly-roll style. Arrange rolls, seam side down, on baking sheet. Refrigerate, covered, until ready to serve. Cut each tortilla crosswise into 4 slices. Secure each slice with toothpick. Top each with whole olive.

12 servings.

SALAMI ROLL-UPS

VICKI HOSS
REDWOOD CITY, CALIFORNIA

1 (8-oz.) pkg. cream cheese, softened

2 tablespoons prepared horseradish

1 lb. sliced salami

❶ In medium bowl, combine cream cheese and horseradish; mix well. Spread cream cheese mixture evenly over salami slices; roll up. Refrigerate, covered, 1 hour before serving.

8 to 12 servings.

WONTON APPETIZERS

NANCY NEWMAN
NIPOMO, CALIFORNIA

WONTONS

48 wonton wrappers

1 tablespoon vegetable oil

SAUSAGE MIXTURE

2 cups cooked crumbled sausage, drained

1½ cups (6 oz.) grated cheddar cheese

1½ cups (6 oz.) grated Monterey Jack cheese

1 cup ranch dressing

½ cup chopped ripe olives

½ cup finely chopped green bell pepper

❶ Heat oven to 350°F. Spray 24 (1¾-inch) miniature muffin cups with nonstick cooking spray.

❷ Brush each wonton wrapper with vegetable oil. Press each wrapper into bottom and up sides of each cup. Bake, uncovered, 7 to 8 minutes or until lightly browned.

❸ In large bowl, combine sausage, cheese, dressing, olives and bell pepper; mix well. Fill each wrapper evenly with sausage mixture. Bake an additional 5 minutes or until heated through.

24 servings.

TORTILLA PINWHEELS

CHRIS McBEE
XENIA, OHIO

1 (8-oz.) container sour cream
1 (8-oz.) pkg. cream cheese, softened
3/4 cup sliced green onions
1/2 cup (2 oz.) finely shredded cheddar cheese
1 tablespoon fresh lime juice
1 tablespoon minced seeded jalapeño chiles
8 to 10 (7-inch) flour tortillas
Salsa or picante sauce

❶ In large bowl, combine sour cream, cream cheese, green onions, cheddar cheese, lime juice and chiles; mix well. Spread mixture evenly over each tortilla; roll up tightly. Wrap in plastic wrap; refrigerate 1 hour before serving. Slice rolls into 1-inch pieces. Serve with salsa or picante sauce.

12 servings.

SMOKED SALMON QUESADILLAS

CONNIE LONG
PALM HARBOR, FLORIDA

3/4 cup cream cheese with chives and onions, softened
8 (6-inch) flour tortillas
8 oz. smoked salmon, coarsely chopped
1/4 teaspoon freshly ground pepper

❶ Spread cream cheese evenly over 4 tortillas. Divide salmon evenly among tortillas. Sprinkle with pepper. Top each portion with 1 tortilla, pressing gently. Heat large skillet over medium-high heat. Cook each quesadilla 2 minutes on each side. Cut each quesadilla into 6 wedges.

12 servings.

GREEN ONION PANCAKES WITH PEANUT SAUCE

YEN YEN NG
MESA, ARIZONA

DOUGH
3 cups all-purpose flour
1 teaspoon salt
1 teaspoon sugar
1/2 teaspoon freshly ground pepper
1 cup finely chopped green onions
1 1/4 cups warm water
2 tablespoons toasted sesame oil
Vegetable oil

PEANUT SAUCE
3/4 cups peanut butter
3 tablespoons low-sodium soy sauce
1 tablespoon fresh lime juice
1 large garlic clove, crushed
1/2 teaspoon curry powder
2 tablespoons packed brown sugar
1 cup coconut milk
1 teaspoon chili-garlic sauce

❶ In large bowl, combine flour, salt, sugar, pepper and green onion; mix well. Gradually add water and sesame oil, stirring with wooden spoon until dough holds together. Turn dough out onto lightly floured board; knead dough 5 minutes or until smooth. Cover dough with clean kitchen towel; let rest 30 minutes.

❷ In small saucepan, combine peanut butter, soy sauce, lime juice, garlic, curry powder, brown sugar, coconut milk and garlic sauce; mix well. Whisk peanut butter mixture over medium-low heat until smooth and hot. Remove from heat; set aside.

❸ On lightly floured board, divide dough into 12 portions. To make pancake, roll portion of dough to make 6-inch circle about 1/8 inch thick.

❹ In small skillet, heat 1 tablespoon oil over medium-high heat until hot. Add pancake; cook 2 to 3 minutes on each side or until golden brown. Remove and drain pancake on paper towel. Add more oil as needed; repeat with remaining pancakes. Cut pancakes into 4 to 8 wedges. Serve warm with peanut sauce.

24 servings.

SHRIMP DUMPLINGS

CAROLYN LYONS
BROCKTON, MASSACHUSETTS

1/2 lb. shelled, deveined cooked medium shrimp, finely chopped

6 water chestnuts, minced

6 mushrooms, finely chopped

1 green onion, finely chopped

1 egg, lightly beaten

1 1/2 tablespoons low-sodium soy sauce

1 tablespoon honey

1/4 teaspoon salt

2 teaspoons sesame oil

36 wonton wrappers

❶ In large bowl, combine shrimp, water chestnuts, mushrooms and green onion; mix well. Stir in egg, soy sauce, honey, salt and oil. Spread 2 teaspoons shrimp mixture evenly into center of each wrapper. Pleat edges up around filling. Press pleats together, leaving top open. Cover to prevent drying.

❷ In wok or large skillet, bring about 1 inch of water to a boil over medium-high heat. Arrange wontons on steamer rack in wok or skillet, open side up, not touching. Reduce heat to low; steam, covered, 10 to 15 minutes or until wontons are transparent. Arrange on a serving dish. Serve warm.

12 servings.

CRAB WONTONS

CINDY HUMPHREYS
KIRKSVILLE, MISSOURI

1 (8-oz.) pkg. cream cheese, softened

1 (6-oz.) can lump crabmeat, drained, flaked

1 tablespoon finely minced green onions

1 1/2 teaspoon fresh lemon juice

1/4 teaspoon garlic powder

1/2 teaspoon salt

1 (1-lb.) pkg. wonton wrappers

Canola oil for frying

❶ In large bowl, combine cream cheese, crabmeat, onions, lemon juice, garlic powder and salt; mix well. Spread 1 teaspoon cream cheese mixture evenly into center of each wrapper. Pull corners to the top; twist to secure.

❷ In large skillet, heat oil to 400°F. Carefully place wontons, twisted end up, in oil; fry 1 minute or until lightly golden. Do not turn upside down while frying. Remove wontons from oil to paper towels; drain.

10 servings.

BACON-CHEESE PUFFS

ANN NACE
PERKASIE, PENNSYLVANIA

6 thin slices bread, crusts removed

12 thick slices bacon, halved (3 inches long)

1 cup (4 oz.) grated cheddar cheese

❶ Heat oven to 400°F.

❷ Cut each bread slice into 4 squares. Place 1 piece of bread in middle of each bacon slice. Sprinkle with cheese. Roll up bacon and bread; secure with toothpick. Place roll-ups on baking sheet. Sprinkle remaining cheese over top. Bake, uncovered, 20 minutes or until bacon is crisp and bread is lightly browned.

8 servings.

MINI CHIMIS

MARK JOHNSON
FREMONT, CALIFORNIA

3/4 lb. ground sirloin

1/2 cup finely chopped onions

1 or 2 tablespoons dry taco seasoning

1 (16-oz.) can refried beans

1 tablespoon chopped green chiles

1 cup (4 oz.) shredded Mexican cheese blend

Vegetable oil for frying

1 (1-lb.) pkg. wonton wrappers

Taco sauce

Sour cream

Guacamole

❶ In large skillet, cook beef and onions over medium-high heat until beef is no longer pink. Stir in taco seasoning; toss to coat evenly. Remove beef mixture from skillet; drain. Return mixture to skillet. Stir in refried beans, green chiles and cheese; stir until blended and cheese begins to melt.

❷ Moisten edges of each wonton with water. Spread 1 teaspoon mixture evenly into corner of each wrapper. Tuck in ends; roll up.

❸ In large skillet or deep fryer, heat oil to 375°F. Add wontons; fry until golden brown and crispy. Drain on paper towels. Serve with taco sauce, sour cream or guacamole.

10 servings.

POT STICKERS

JULIE OSTROM
CHIPPEWA FALLS, WISCONSIN

1/2 cup very finely chopped Chinese (napa) cabbage, drained

8 oz. lean ground pork

2 tablespoons finely chopped water chestnuts

1 green onion, finely chopped

1 1/2 teaspoons low-sodium soy sauce

1 1/2 teaspoons dry sherry

1/2 teaspoon minced fresh ginger

1 1/2 teaspoons cornstarch

1/2 teaspoon sesame oil

1/4 teaspoon sugar

1 (12-oz.) pkg. pot sticker wrappers

2 tablespoons vegetable oil

2/3 cup canned reduced-sodium chicken broth

1/2 cup low-sodium soy sauce

1/2 cup vinegar cider or Chinese vinegar

1 teaspoon chili oil

❶ In large bowl, combine cabbage, pork, water chestnuts, green onion, soy sauce, sherry, ginger, cornstarch, sesame oil and sugar; mix well. Spread 1 teaspoon filling evenly into center of each wrapper. To shape, lightly moisten edges of dough circle with water; fold in half. Starting at end, pinch curled edges together making 4 pleats along edge.

❷ In large saucepan, heat oil over medium-high heat until hot. Add wontons, seam side up; cook over medium-high heat 5 to 6 minutes or until bottoms are golden brown. Pour in chicken broth. Cover tightly, reduce heat to medium; cook 10 minutes or until all liquid is absorbed and pork is no longer pink. Place wontons, browned-side up, on serving platter. Serve with mixture of soy sauce, vinegar and chili oil for dipping.

10 servings.

SANTA FE ROLL-UPS

DAVID HEPPNER
BRANDON, FLORIDA

SPREAD
1 (15-oz.) can black-eyed peas, rinsed, drained
¼ cup coarsely chopped onions
4 oz. reduced-fat cream cheese, softened
1 tablespoon ketchup
1 tablespoon canned diced green chiles
1½ teaspoon chili powder
½ teaspoon ground cumin
½ teaspoon finely chopped garlic
⅛ teaspoon freshly ground pepper

FILLING
⅔ cup frozen whole kernel corn, cooked, drained
⅓ cup chopped green bell peppers
⅓ cup chopped red bell peppers
½ cup finely chopped red onions
¼ cup chopped fresh cilantro
1 tablespoon canned diced jalapeño chiles, if desired
6 (10-inch) flour tortillas

❶ In food processor, combine ¾ cup of the black-eyed peas, onions, cream cheese, ketchup, green chiles, chili powder, cumin, garlic and pepper; process until smooth.

❷ In medium bowl, combine remaining ¼ cup black-eyed peas with corn, bell peppers, onions, cilantro and chiles; mix well. Spread 3 tablespoons cream cheese mixture evenly over each tortilla. Sprinkle with ⅓ cup filling; roll up tortillas, jelly roll style. Wrap tightly in plastic wrap. Refrigerate 1 hour. To serve, slice and discard ends of tortillas. Slice each roll into 6 pieces.

12 servings.

SPINACH-MUSHROOM QUESADILLAS

ALICE HOFFMAN
BALTIMORE, MARYLAND

2 tablespoons butter
2 garlic cloves, minced
⅔ cup finely chopped onions
8 oz. fresh button mushrooms, sliced
1 (10-oz.) package frozen chopped spinach, thawed, drained
⅓ cup chopped fresh parsley
½ teaspoon nutmeg
2½ cups (10 oz.) grated Monterey Jack cheese
⅛ teaspoon salt
⅛ teaspoon freshly ground pepper
¼ cup olive oil
16 (5½-inch) tortillas

❶ In large skillet, melt butter over medium-high heat. Add garlic, onions and mushrooms; sauté until tender, but not brown. Remove garlic mixture from heat to large clean bowl; set aside.

❷ Stir spinach, parsley and nutmeg into garlic mixture. Add 2 cups of the cheese; mix thoroughly. Season with salt and pepper.

❸ Heat oven to 350°F. Brush oil evenly over each tortilla. Place tortillas, oiled-side down, on pizza stone or baking sheet. Divide garlic mixture equally among tortillas, spreading to edges of tortilla. Top with remaining 8 tortillas, pressing down slightly. Brush tops with olive oil, then sprinkle with remaining cheese. Bake, uncovered, 10 minutes or until heated through and cheese has melted. Cut into wedges and serve.

16 servings.

ORIENTAL ROLLS

TERESA WORTH
BOISE, IDAHO

2 tablespoons vegetable oil, plus more for frying

¾ lb. ground pork

¼ lb. shelled, deveined uncooked medium shrimp

1 medium onion

2 teaspoons five-spice powder

4 tablespoons sesame seeds

1 (1-lb.) pkg. wonton wrappers

❶ In food processor, combine pork, shrimp, onion and five-spice powder; process until well blended and finely ground. In medium skillet, heat 2 tablespoons oil over medium-high heat until hot. Add pork mixture; sauté 3 to 5 minutes or until pork is no longer pink in center.

❷ Spoon about 1 tablespoon mixture evenly into each wrapper; roll up tightly. Wet edges slightly to seal. Dip each end into dish of sesame seeds.

❸ In large skillet, wok or deep fryer, heat oil to 400°F. Add wontons to skillet; fry 5 or 6 at a time 3 to 4 minutes or until golden brown. Drain and serve hot. Store up to 72 hours.

20 servings.

OLIVE BALLS

NANCY MARTIN GUICE
LAUREL, MISSISSIPPI

1 (8-oz.) can refrigerated crescent roll dough

24 green pimiento-stuffed olives

2 tablespoons melted butter

❶ Heat oven to 375°F. Unroll dough. Cut each triangle in three triangles. Brush or spray with butter. Place 1 olive in center of each triangle; roll up like a crescent roll. Brush top with butter. Bake, uncovered, 7 to 9 minutes or until golden brown.

12 servings.

SMOKED SALMON ROLL-UPS

LORNA HOUSE
FREDERICK, MARYLAND

5 (10-inch) flour tortillas

1 (8-oz.) pkg. cream cheese, softened

3 tablespoons mayonnaise

1 tablespoon chopped fresh parsley

1 tablespoon finely chopped green onions

2 tablespoons prepared horseradish

3 oz. smoked salmon, coarsely chopped

⅛ teaspoon salt

⅛ teaspoon freshly ground pepper

Fresh parsley

❶ In food processor, combine cream cheese and mayonnaise until smooth. Add parsley, green onions and horseradish; process until mixture is of spreading consistency. (*If it is too thick, thin with milk 1 teaspoon at a time until it reaches spreading consistency.*)

❷ Transfer mixture to large bowl; fold in salmon. Season with salt and pepper. Spread mixture evenly over each tortilla. Roll up tightly into log, being careful not to break or tear tortilla; trim off ends. Tightly wrap each tortilla in plastic wrap; refrigerate 8 hours or until firm enough to slice.

❸ Slice each tortilla diagonally into bite-size pieces (*approximately 7 to 8 slices per tortilla.*) Arrange on serving platter. Garnish with parsley.

12 servings.

PINEAPPLE ROLL-UPS

**KIMBERLY RAY
HOUSTON, TEXAS**

18 thin slices white bread, crusts removed

1 (8-oz.) pkg. cream cheese, softened

1 egg yolk, beaten

1 cup plus 2 tablespoons sugar

1 tablespoon vanilla

1/2 cup drained crushed pineapple

1/2 cup butter, melted

1 teaspoon cinnamon

❶ Heat oven to 350°F. Spray baking sheet with non-stick cooking spray.

❷ Roll bread slices flat with rolling pin. In medium bowl, combine cream cheese, egg yolk, 2 tablespoons of the sugar and vanilla; mix well until creamy. Fold in pineapple. Spread 1 tablespoon of mixture evenly over each side of bread. Roll up; cut into fourths.

❸ In small bowl, combine cinnamon and remaining 1 cup sugar; mix well. Dip roll-ups in butter, then roll in cinnamon mixture. Arrange roll-ups on baking sheet. Bake, uncovered, 10 minutes.

18 servings.

GREEN ONION ROLL-UPS

**FRANCES KIRCHEM
FT. WORTH, TEXAS**

1 (8-oz.) container reduced-fat jalapeño-flavored cream cheese, softened

3 (2.5-oz.) pkg. lean thin-sliced lunch meats, such as ham, beef and turkey

4 bunches green onions, trimmed

❶ Spread cream cheese evenly over each slice of meat. Place 1 green onion on each side; roll up. Secure with toothpick. Keep refrigerated until ready to serve.

12 servings.

MINI SAUSAGE TURNOVERS

**ANGIE STEPHENSON
BOONE, IOWA**

1 lb. frozen bread dough, thawed

4 oz. bulk Italian sausage

1/4 cup chopped onions

1/4 teaspoon garlic salt

1/4 teaspoon dried basil

1/4 teaspoon dried oregano

1/2 cup tomato sauce

1/2 cup (2 oz.) shredded mozzarella cheese

1 egg, beaten

❶ Divide dough into 8 portions.

❷ Heat large skillet over medium heat. Add sausage; cook until sausage is crumbled and no longer pink; drain. Stir in onions, garlic salt, basil, oregano and tomato sauce; simmer 10 minutes.

❸ Heat oven to 425°F. Spray baking sheet with non-stick cooking spray.

❹ Roll each dough piece into 5-inch circle. Spoon sausage mixture over each circle; sprinkle with cheese. Moisten edges of dough with water. Fold dough over to enclose filling; press with fork to seal. Place on baking sheet. Brush egg over turnovers. Bake, uncovered, 10 to 15 minutes or until golden brown. Serve hot.

8 servings.

Recipe Index

General Index